THE
CONNOISSEUR'S GUIDE TO
COFFEE

DISCOVER THE WORLD'S MOST
EXQUISITE COFFEE BEANS

Jon Thorn
and
Michael Segal

THE
CONNOISSEUR'S GUIDE TO
COFFEE

DISCOVER THE WORLD'S MOST
EXQUISITE COFFEE BEANS

Jon Thorn
and
Michael Segal

APPLE

A QUINTET BOOK

First published in the UK in 2007 by
Apple Press
7 Greenland Street
London NW1 0ND
United Kingdom

www.apple-press.com

Reprinted in 2010

ISBN: 978-1-84543-143-3

This book was designed and produced by
Quintet Publishing Limited
6 Blundell Street
London N7 9BH

Project Editor Second Edition: **Victoria Wiggins**
Project Editor First Edition: **Laura Sandelson**
Designers: **Rod Teasdale & Emma Teasdale**
Photographer: **Paul Forrester**
Illustrator: **Katy Sleight**
Creative Director: **Richard Dewing**
Managing Editor: **Jane Laing**
Publisher: **Judith More**

Manufactured in Singapore by Pica Digital Pte. Ltd.
Printed in China by Toppan Leefung Printers Ltd.

CONTENTS

Coffee is the common man's gold, and like gold,
it brings to every man the feeling of luxury
and nobility.
Abd-al-Kadir (1587)

When you are worried, have trouble of one sort
or another—to the coffee house!
Peter Altenberg (1922)

Complacencies of the peignoir, and late
Coffee and oranges in a sunny chair,
And the green freedom of a cockatoo
Upon a rug mingle to dissipate
The holy hush of ancient sacrifice.
"Sunday Morning"
Wallace Stevens (1923)

I have measured out my life with coffee spoons.
from "The Love Song of J. Alfred Prufrock"
T. S. Eliot (1917)

Interior of a café at Constantinople.

THE STORY OF COFFEE

THE SECRET SPREADS

Nineteenth century painting of a coffee house, Constantinople.

The coffee plant originated in Ethiopia and the Horn of Africa, where it grows wild even today, but it was in the country now known as Yemen (formerly Arabia) that the diffusion and horticultural propagation of coffee began. In those days Yemen was one of the busiest places in the world, with Mocha, the country's main port, at its center.

Some authorities say that the cultivation of coffee began in Yemen in AD 575, but it was certainly highly developed there by the fifteenth century. From Yemen, coffee began its great journey around the world. Just as tea was a jealously guarded commodity in China, so was coffee regarded by the Arabs. Coffee beans are the seeds of the coffee plant; when stripped of their outer cherry and husk, they become infertile. It was only in this form that they were allowed to be exported from Arabia.

Coffee's path from Arabia mirrors to some extent the route that tradition claims coffee followed to arrive in Arabia in the first place.

One story tells how black Sudanese slaves were brought through Ethiopia en route to Arabia. They took with them supplies of coffee, still in its red cherry coverings, to help them survive the journey, and it was in this way that coffee cherries were carried to Arabia.

It was inevitable that travelers to Mecca, at the heart of the Muslim world, would carry some of the beans with them. One legend recounts that the Arabs themselves took coffee to Sri Lanka (previously Ceylon) as early as 1505; however, the man most widely credited with spreading coffee to the East is one Baba Budan, who returned from pilgrimage to Mecca to his home in southwest India with some fertile beans at some point in the seventeenth century.

By the early 1600s, German, French, Italian, and Dutch traders were vying with each other to introduce coffee to their overseas colonies. The Dutch triumphed in 1616 when a coffee plant was taken via Mocha to The Netherlands, and by 1658 the Dutch were cultivating coffee in Sri Lanka.

In 1670, one of coffee's great failures occurred. Some French optimists, who had somehow obtained several plants, attempted to establish a plantation near Dijon, an area notable for its cold winters and freezing fogs. It is a mystery why this group thought that coffee plants, which prospered in Arabia but could only be grown in The Netherlands in heated glasshouses, would flourish in open fields in central France.

One of the key figures in the history of coffee is the Burgermeister of Amsterdam, Nicolaas Witson. In 1696, Witson suggested to Adrian van Ommen, the commander at Malabar, that coffee be taken to Java (then a Dutch possession), and seeds were planted accordingly at the Kedawoeng Estate, Batavia. Unfortunately, these early seedlings were washed away. Three years later, Henricus Zwaaydecroon took cuttings from Malabar to Java and successfully transplanted them. Thus began the first European plantation, and the profits it quickly brought encouraged others.

In 1706, the first samples of Java coffee were sent to Amsterdam, along with a coffee plant, which was nurtured in the city's botanical gardens. Seeds from the plant were generously distributed to horticultural enthusiasts throughout Europe. Meanwhile, the Dutch were expanding production into Sumatra and the Celebes (now Sulawesi) in the Indonesian archipelago, and Indonesia was the world's first commercial exporter of coffee. Today it is the fourth largest producer and exporter.

Attempts to transfer coffee plants between The Netherlands and France failed until, in 1714, a tree 5 feet (1.5 meters) tall was sent from Amsterdam to Louis XIV of France. This tree, which was transferred to the Jardin des Plantes in Paris, is the identifiable

Nearly all the coffee plants grown in the French colonies can be traced back to the tree given to Louis XIV in 1714.

ancestor of the first coffee plants grown in most of the French colonies, and in South and Central America and the Caribbean. In 1715, coffee plants were taken to Bourbon (now known as La Réunion), and soon this tiny island began to export coffee. From one tree, coffee production began to spread.

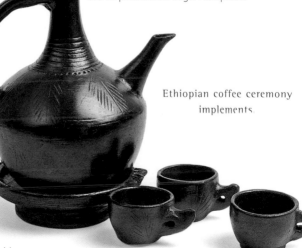

Ethiopian coffee ceremony implements

GABRIEL MATHIEU DE CLIEU

One of the most romantic of the stories associated with coffee is that of Gabriel Mathieu de Clieu, a French naval officer serving in Martinique in the eighteenth century. While he was on leave in Paris, de Clieu succeeded in obtaining some coffee plants that he determined to take back to Martinique. This may have been in 1720 or in 1723; or he may have made the journey twice because the first consignment died. What is certain is that de Clieu eventually set sail from Nantes with the most famous and best cared for plant of all time. The plant was stowed on deck in a glass box to protect it from salt spray and to keep it warm.

De Clieu's journal tells how the ship was threatened by pirates from Tunis and how it survived a violent storm. It also reveals that de Clieu had an enemy on board who was jealous of his mission and tried to sabotage the plant, even tearing off a branch in one struggle. The ship was then becalmed and drinking water became short. The selfless de Clieu shared his own water ration with the plant.

Finally de Clieu arrived safely in Martinique and the coffee tree was planted at Prechear, surrounded by thorn bushes and kept under round-the-clock watch by slaves. It thrived and multiplied, and by 1726 the first harvest was gathered. We are told that by 1777 there were 18,791,680 coffee plants on Martinique, from where plants were sent to Haiti, Santo Domingo, and Guadeloupe.

Sadly, de Clieu did not live to see this triumph. He died in Paris, an honored if not a wealthy man, on November 30, 1724, at the age of 88. He is commemorated by a memorial, which was erected in 1918 in the botanical garden of the Fort de France on Martinique.

Gabriel Mathieu de Clieu with the first coffee plant
on his way to Martinique.

COFFEE TRAVELS EAST AND WEST

It was not until 1718, when the Dutch took plants to Surinam—their colony on the northeast coast of South America—that coffee arrived on the continent that quickly became the coffee center of the world. There soon followed the establishment of the first plantation in Para, Brazil, in 1727, with plants taken from French Guiana. These were followed by a different variety, from the Portuguese Indian colony of Goa, which was planted around Rio de Janeiro. In 1730, the British introduced coffee to Jamaica, initiating the long and fascinating history of Blue Mountain coffee there. Then, between 1750 and 1760, coffee was first grown in Guatemala. Nearly two decades later, Don Francisco Xavier Navarro took plants from Cuba to Costa Rica, and in 1790, coffee was first grown in Mexico. In 1825, seeds from the plantation around Rio de Janeiro were taken to Hawaii, where coffee is still grown today—the only genuine U.S. coffee.

In 1878, the story came almost full circle when the foundations of the Kenyan coffee industry were laid by British settlers who introduced coffee plants to British East Africa, augmented in 1901 by plants from La Réunion. In 1887, the French established a plantation in Tonkin (now Vietnam), and in 1896, coffee trees were planted in Queensland, Australia.

In this way, the secret that the Arabs had so long sought to keep eventually spread throughout the world.

THE FIRST COFFEE HOUSES

We do not know who the earliest coffee drinkers were, but it is almost certain that they lived in Ethiopia. References to a beverage known as "buncham"—that may or may not be coffee—are found in Arabic scientific documents dating from AD 900 to AD 1000, although these documents are largely focused on the scientific qualities of the bean.

In addition to describing the benefits to "the stomache, the members, the skin," the writers note that the drink gives "an excellent smell to the whole body." It is true that coffee has the unusual quality of appearing to retain its aroma through the sweat glands. In the days before baths were taken regularly and in areas where water was a scarce resource, this deodorant effect must have been greatly appreciated.

An Arab legend, dating from around 1250, tells how the exiled Sheikh Omar discovered coffee berries growing wild. Hungry and bored with eating the raw beans, the sheikh is said to have boiled some of the berries and drunk the resulting brew. This was not only a welcome change in the sheikh's diet; when he administered the liquid to some infirm people, they recovered. The sheikh returned home in triumph from his exile in Mocha, carrying some of the precious beans with him. There are several versions of this tale, and virtually the only element they have in common is the name Omar. Other variants include ghosts; the curing of the beautiful daughter of the king of Mocha; and the ravishing song of a wondrous bird, which disappeared after leading Omar to a tree laden with coffee fruits.

One of the most common legends is that of a goatherd in Arabia—or possibly Egypt, or even somewhere else entirely—who noticed that his goats became livelier after eating coffee berries. He reported his findings to the local abbot, who

An Arab woman prepares coffee in the
traditional Arabic style.

experimented on his monks. They soon found
that the brew helped them stay awake
throughout their nightly prayers.

In the last 200 years, researchers into the
origins of coffee have come to some curious
conclusions. One writer believes that coffee
existed in the time of Homer and that it was the
"wondrous drink" that Helen took with her from
Sparta to Troy. Yet another writer has concluded
that King David received coffee from Abigail and
that both Esau and Ruth drank it.

It is recorded that in 1454, the Mufti of Aden
visited Ethiopia and saw his own countrymen
drinking coffee there. When he returned home,
he sent for some beans, and not only did the
beverage cure him of an affliction but the Mufti
noted its ability to keep him awake. It quickly
became popular with the dervishes.

Coffee drinking and cultivation in Yemen
certainly predated 1454. In that year, it was
approved by the government, which may have
felt that the invigorating qualities of coffee were
preferable to the soporific qualities of *qat* (or
kat)—a plant whose leaves were (and still are)
widely grown and used throughout the country.

It was in Mecca that the first coffee houses,
known as Kaveh Kanes, were established, and
although they were originally religious in
purpose, they quickly developed into centers of
chess, gossip, singing, dancing, and music. From
Mecca they spread to Aden, Medina, and Cairo.

Coffee was taken to Constantinople in 1517
after Salim I had conquered Egypt. From there,
the habit of coffee drinking spread throughout
the area, becoming established in Damascus by
1530 and in Aleppo by 1532. Two of the best-
known coffee houses in Damascus were the
Café of the Roses and the Café of the Gate of
Salvation. Although coffee houses were not seen
in Constantinople itself until 1554, they soon
became famous for their luxurious furnishings,
as owners competed with each other to attract
customers. They became meeting places for both
social and business occasions and, increasingly,
the home of heated political debate and dissent.
Despite several attempts to impose a ban on
coffee—at one stage second offenders were
sewn into a leather bag and thrown into the
Bosphorus—its respectability was assured when
it became subject to tax.

EUROPEAN COFFEE HOUSES

It is easy for us to forget why coffee houses
proved to be so popular both in the Middle East
and Europe. Quite simply, nothing like them had
ever existed before. Before the advent of the
coffee house, there had been nowhere to enjoy
a pleasant, relatively inexpensive drink in
convivial company. Coffee finally arrived in
Europe in 1615, having been brought by
Venetian traders. This was several years later
than tea, which was first sold in Europe in 1610,
and many years after cocoa, which was brought
from the New World by the Spanish in 1528.

When coffee was first seen in Italy, some
clerics demanded for it to be excommunicated
because it must be the Devil's work. The pope,

Clement VIII (1592–1605), decided to see for himself, and he enjoyed the cup so much that he declared instead that "coffee should be baptized to make it a true Christian drink."

Initially coffee was regarded as a medicine, and it commanded a high price. It was also largely sold by lemonade vendors. As far as can be determined, the first coffee house—*bottega del caffè*—was opened in Venice in 1683, although one unsubstantiated claim suggests that it was 1645. Caffè Florian in the Piazza San Marco—one of the best known and, outside Japan, most expensive coffee houses in the world—was opened by Floriano Francescari in 1720. Coffee houses in Italy are still called caffès; elsewhere in Europe they are called cafés.

Thereafter, coffee houses proliferated throughout Italy, although most were in Venice. Giorgio Quadri, the first proprietor to offer authentic Turkish coffee, opened his coffee shop in 1775, and this was quickly followed by Due di Toscania, Imperatore Imperatrice della Russia,

Tamerlano, Fantae di Diana, Dame Venete, Pace, and Arabo-Piastrelle.

The first coffee house in England was opened not in London but in Oxford, in 1650, by a man called Jacob. About four years later a second coffee house, Cirques Johnson, was opened in Oxford—according to some sources, also by a man called Jacob. A coffee club that started in a private house near to All Souls' College later became the Royal Society.

The first coffee house in London was opened in 1652 in St Michael's Alley, Cornhill, and was owned by Pasqua Rosee, who may have been Greek, and a Mr Bowman. This became the model for many of the coffee houses that subsequently opened; one of the best known of which was Mol's Coffee House in Exeter, Devon. The most famous survivor of all the London coffee houses was that founded—originally in Tower Street and later in Lombard Street—by Edward Lloyd in 1688. As a service to his customers, Lloyd used to prepare lists of

Caffè Florian, in Venice, is Europe's oldest surviving coffee house.

the ships that his clients had insured, and eventually Lloyd's became the largest single insurance house in the world.

NORTH AMERICAN COFFEE HOUSES

The first reference to coffee in North America dates from 1668, when it is described as being drunk with sugar or honey and cinnamon. Soon after this, however, coffee houses were established in New York, Philadelphia, Boston, and other towns.

In Boston, the two earliest coffee houses were the London Coffee House and the Gutteridge Coffee House, which opened in 1691, and one of the most famous was the Green Dragon, where the Boston Tea Party was planned in 1773. Boston also became the site of the largest, most expensive, and grandest coffee-exchange house in the world when, in 1808, a seven-storey building, costing $50,000, was built on the model of Lloyd's of London. It was destroyed by fire only 10 years later.

In New York, where coffee quickly replaced "must" (a kind of beer) as the most popular breakfast drink, the main market for green beans was established in 1683. William Penn sent his orders for beans from Pennsylvania to New York. The first coffee house to appear in the city was the King's Arms, which opened in 1696. This was followed by the Exchange Coffee House in Broad Street, which was built in 1730 and became a major trading center. The Exchange was later eclipsed by the Merchants' Coffee House, and it was here that the Bank of New York was formed in 1784 and where the first stocks were sold in 1790. The Tontine, on Wall and Water Streets in New York, was the headquarters of the New York Stock Exchange for 10 years.

In Philadelphia, the third great city of early American history, the first coffee house was opened in 1700. It was simply called Ye Coffee House, and its main competitor was the London Coffee House.

Coffee houses in the United States differed from their European counterparts, tending to be centers for conservative elements rather than for radicals, republicans, or the literati. They also often served as the venue for trials and council meetings in cities where there were few civic buildings.

An illustration of Lloyd's coffee house, London, by William Holland, c.1798.

WHAT IS COFFEE?

Drawing of *Coffea*, showing both flowers and fruit.

Our word "coffee" comes from the Latin name of the genus *Coffea*. The genus is a member of the Rubiaceae family, which includes more than 500 genera and 6,000 species, most of which are tropical trees and shrubs.

The eighteenth-century Swedish botanist, Carolus Linnaeus, described the genus, but botanists are still not in complete agreement on the precise classification. There are probably at least 25 major species within the genus—all indigenous to tropical Africa and some islands in the Indian Ocean—but problems have arisen because of the wide variations that occur in the plants and seeds. All species of *Coffea* are woody, but they can be small shrubs or tall trees more than 32 feet (10 meters) high. The leaves range in color from yellowish to purple.

From the coffee drinker's point of view, there are two major and two lesser species within the genus. *Coffea arabica*, which Linnaeus identified in 1753, gives us arabica beans, the quality coffee of the world. Arabica coffees are described as "Brazils," which come from Brazil, and "Other Milds," which come from elsewhere. *Coffea canephora* or, more accurately, *C. canephora* var. *robusta*, provides the robusta beans, a hardier type that are often used to make arabica go further. The two minor species within the genus are *C. liberica* and *C. excelsa* (*C. dewevrei*), which give the little-used liberica and excelsa beans respectively.

The two best-known varieties of *C. arabica* are Typica and Bourbon, but many strains have been developed, including Caturra (which is grown in Brazil and Colombia), Mundo Novo (also from Brazil), Tico (which is widely grown in Central America), San Ramon (a dwarf strain), and, perhaps most famously, Jamaica Blue

Coffee cherries ripening on a branch.

proportion of robusta is increasing—largely because of the better yields that are possible from robusta trees. In addition, arabica trees are more prone to disease than plants producing robusta beans.

Both arabica and robusta trees produce a crop 3 to 4 years after planting, and they are viable for between 20 and 30 years, depending on conditions and care. Thereafter, they must be replaced. Both species require plenty of sun and rain. Arabica trees prefer a seasonal climate with a temperature range of 59 to 75°F (15 to 24°C); robusta prefers warm, equatorial conditions with more constant temperatures of between 75 and 85°F (24 and 29°C). Both species die when the temperature falls below freezing—although the arabica trees are hardier—and both require an annual rainfall of 60 inches (150 centimeters).

The traditional way to grow coffee is under suitable trees in the surrounding area, which shade the coffee and its developing fruit from the hottest sun. As well as limiting the damage that may be caused by direct sun, the shade of other trees helps to conserve the moisture in the soil. A more modern technique is to use irrigation and fertilizers, which require investment and which must, therefore, be economic in terms of yield and added value; as a result, they are really only viable in commercial plantations.

Coffee is grown on very large estates and in the smallest of forest clearings, and on almost every size of farm and smallholding between. In Brazil and Guatemala, for example, there are many large estates devoted to growing nothing but coffee, and in Brazil in particular mechanical harvesters are increasingly used. The large estates can produce high yields, but they also have high input and capital costs; smaller farms have lower yields but lower costs.

The main variables in coffee production are the labor and land costs. Higher labor costs can be offset by using modern methods, including the use of fertilizers, herbicides and pesticides, mechanization, and irrigation. But all of these require investment.

Mountain. The average arabica plant is a large bush with dark-green, oval leaves. The fruits—bright-red, so-called cherries—are also oval and usually contain two flattish seeds: the "beans" themselves. Robusta plants are shrubs or small trees that grow to as much as 32 feet (10 meters) or more in height, but with a shallow root system. The fruits are round and take up to 11 months to mature. The seeds are oval and somewhat smaller than the arabica beans. Robusta coffee is grown in West and Central Africa, throughout Southeast Asia and in Brazil, where it is known as Conillon.

At present arabica coffee represents around two-thirds of the world's production, but the

HARVESTING THE BEANS

After three or four years, when they come to maturity, the coffee trees bear fruit, which is borne in lines or clusters along the branches of the trees.

The beans that we see are, of course, the seeds of the coffee tree. The seeds are surrounded by a fruit—or "cherry"—which turns red when it is ready to be harvested. Beneath the red skin, the exocarp, there is a fleshy pulp, the mesocarp, then a slimy layer, then a parchment-like covering of the bean, the endocarp. Inside these layers are, usually, two beans, flat sides facing each other, and the beans are covered in a thin membrane or coat.

Most coffee cherries ripen to a bright, lustrous red, although some varieties are bright yellow at maturity. Arabica cherries ripen after 6 to 8 months; robusta takes 9 to 11 months. There can, therefore, really be only one harvest a year, although in countries in which the division between the wet and dry seasons is not clearly defined—Colombia and Kenya, for example— there may be two flowerings a year, therefore permitting a main and a secondary crop.

Harvest times vary according to geographical zone. North of the Equator— such as in Ethiopia and Central America—the harvest takes place between September and December. South of the Equator—in Brazil and Zimbabwe, for instance— the main harvest is in April or May, although it may last until August. Equatorial countries— such as Uganda and Colombia—can harvest fruit all year round, especially if plantations take advantage of different altitudes. It is possible, therefore, for there to be freshly harvested beans for much of the year.

The harvesting can be done—by hand or by machine—in one of two ways. The first is strip picking, in which the entire crop is picked in one pass through the plantation. The other method,

Coffee plantation, Bali, Indonesia.

Freshly harvested coffee cherries are gathered, Costa Rica.

selective picking, involves making several passes at intervals of 8 to 10 days among the trees so that only the red, fully ripe berries are taken. Selective picking is, clearly, more expensive and labor intensive than strip picking, and it is only employed for arabica trees, especially if that coffee is to be wet processed (see page 20).

The number of cherries picked will be determined by a variety of factors, the most obvious of which are the size of the trees and the layout of the farm or plantation. On an average farm, a picker would probably pick between 110 to 220 pounds (50 and 100 kilograms) of cherries a day. Of this total weight, however, only 20 percent is actually bean, so the daily yield per picker is 22 to 44 pounds (10 to 20 kilograms). Coffee is supplied in standard bags of 100 or 130 pounds (45 or 60 kilograms). Therefore, it takes one picker between three and six days to fill one bag.

It is estimated that the costs of harvesting represent about half the total annual costs of a coffee plantation or farm. In Brazil, attempts have been made to reduce these costs by introducing mechanical pickers, which straddle the coffee trees and shake the branches so that the loose, ripe berries fall into hoppers. Mechanical harvesters are only suitable on soft, unchallenging terrain, and they require forward planning, for they are useful only where the trees are planted in straight lines. In addition, a mechanically harvested crop will need screening to remove the leaves and twigs that fall into the hopper.

The vast majority of coffee is, therefore, harvested by hand. As well as being intensely seasonal work, the pickers also have to be aware that immature, diseased, or overripe cherries should be avoided, as they will affect the final quality of the rest of the product.

PROCESSING THE BEANS

There are two ways of preparing coffee beans for roasting, and the method used has a significant effect on the price and quality of the final beans. The cheapest process is known as the "dry" method, which is normally used for lower grade beans; the better beans are processed by the "wet" method. Brazil has recently found success with an intermediate method of processing, which has resulted in some beans being termed "semi-washed," or "pulped naturals."

The dry method produces "naturals" or unwashed coffee, while the wet method results in fully washed or semi-washed beans. Most arabica beans are wet processed, as they require more investment and greater care—with the exception of those from Brazil and Ethiopia, where the dry method is more common. In Indonesia some robusta beans are wet processed, although this is unusual. In recent years, robusta producers in origins like India have successfully added value to their crop by using wet processing as well.

THE DRY METHOD

The dry method of processing coffee is the simplest, cheapest, and most traditional. The harvested cherries are spread over a concrete, brick, or matting surface, ideally in sunlight, and the cherries are raked over at regular intervals to prevent fermentation. If it rains or if the temperature falls, the cherries have to be covered to protect them.

After about four weeks, when the moisture content of each cherry will have fallen to about 12 percent, the cherries are dry. By now, the outer shell will have become dark brown and brittle, and you can actually hear the beans rattling around inside the husk.

This process requires more skill than is apparent, for it is possible to over dry the beans; if that happens, they are more likely to be damaged during the next stage, hulling. At the same time, beans that are not sufficiently dry are more susceptible to fungal attack. The dried cherries are then stored in silos, during which time the green beans continue to lose moisture.

Raking the coffee parchment to dry it in the sun, El Salvador.

THE WET METHOD

The wet process requires greater investment and more care, but it helps to preserve the intrinsic qualities of the bean and causes less damage. The main difference between the two methods is that in the wet method the pulp is removed from the bean almost immediately, instead of allowing the cherries to dry first.

The pulp is removed in a pulping machine, which crushes the cherries; either between one fixed and one moving surface or in a machine with adjustable blades. In order to preserve the quality of the beans, pulping has to be done as soon after harvesting as possible—certainly no longer than 24 hours, although before 12 hours have elapsed is ideal. If the beans are left for too long before processing, the pulpy flesh becomes more difficult to separate from the beans, leading to imperfect separation and possible damage to the bean.

The beans, now in their husks, are separated from the skin and pulp, which are washed away with water. The washing channels are designed to separate the lighter, immature beans from the heavier, mature ones, although this separation can also be achieved by means of an Aagaard pre-grader. Aagaard was a Norwegian coffee grower who, when working in Kenya, devised a system that involved shaking the beans through a sieve into a tank of water. The larger, heavier beans sink through the water first; the lighter beans are carried further along into the tank. The water in this process can be recycled. This system produces high-quality, well-pulped, and uniform-size parchment.

The next stage is the essential fermentation—that is, the separation of the slippery mucilage covering the parchment by the action of enzymes. The beans are stored in fermentation tanks for between 12 and 36 hours, depending on the ambient temperature, the thickness of the layer of mucilage, and the enzymes present. When the process is complete, the parchment surrounding the bean is no longer slimy but has a "pebbly" feel.

Pulping the cherries.

Quality control throughout the wet method is essential to prevent a "stinker" bean developing. Even one bean that has been allowed to rot can ruin a whole consignment. For this reason all the equipment used is cleaned daily to ensure nothing is left before the next batch is processed.

Drying the coffee beans on racks, Kenya.

DRYING THE BEANS

The beans are still in their parchment casing, and after the wet method of processing, these casings contain approximately 50 percent moisture. The parchment has to be dried to about 11 percent moisture so that the beans can be stored in a stable condition. This degree of moisture is critical, because if arabica beans are over-dried to 10 percent, they lose their blue-green color and some quality. Too much moisture, on the other hand, promotes mold and endangers bean quality.

The parchment is dried by the sun, after spreading the beans on concrete or paved patios or on drying tables or trays, as for the dry method. Mechanical dryers are available and are used on some of the larger plantations or where rain could spoil the drying. In this case, the beans are placed in conditioning bins and dry air is blown over them. Otherwise, in most cases, the drying is left to the sun. The beans are turned regularly to ensure that they dry evenly, and the process takes between 12 and 15 days.

It is important that the parchment does not crack, so if the sun is too strong, the beans have to be covered.

At this stage the processing is complete and the beans are known as "parchment coffee." Ideally, they will remain in this form until immediately before export.

Because producing countries need to export around the year and not just in the three or so months of the harvesting period, the stored parchment coffee remains in an absolutely stable atmosphere. High humidity is the enemy of coffee and an ambient humidity of 70 percent could easily damage the beans. For this reason, parchment coffee is often not stored on the farms that produced it, although in some areas there may be no alternative. High-grown coffee should be stored at the same or similar altitude as that at which it was grown because it is particularly susceptible to humidity. Arabica beans in this condition should not be stored for more than 12 months; however, robusta beans can be stored for a little longer.

THE SEMI-WASHED ALTERNATIVE

Some coffee-producing origin countries, notably Brazil and India, have recently had great success with an intermediate processing system, the semi-washed method. In Brazil, where this process was first used in the 1990s, the resulting beans are called "pulped naturals"—a term which pretty much describes what the method does. A sort of hybrid between the wet and dry methods of processing, the semi-washed method involves pulping the cherries (as in the wet method), but then allowing the remaining fruit to dry on the beans (as in the dry method), rather than washing.

The resulting coffee benefits from a transfer of some of the drying fruit into the beans, giving increased body and sweetness. This method can also smooth out the earthy notes of some of the traditional natural (dry method) coffees from Brazil.

HULLING

Just before it is exported the coffee will be hulled, which means that the parchment is removed—from both arabica and robusta beans—and the beans are prepared for sale.

It is more difficult to remove the parchment from wet-processed coffee than from dry-processed beans, and different hullers are used. There are two main types: friction hullers and impact hullers. Friction hullers of the Engelberg or Africa type can process both wet and dry method beans. These have a cylindrical casing, and the beans are squeezed between a wire rib and a knife, which shatters the parchment and releases the beans.

Impact hullers, which—except in Brazil—are used only for parchment coffees, do not use friction. The coffee must have the correct moisture content or the beans will break. These hullers consist of a horizontal disk spinning in a circular chamber. Around the edge of the disk are steel pins or bars, and the beans are forced into contact with the pins by centrifugal force. The parchment shells shatter on contact.

POLISHING

Any covering silverskin that remains on the beans after hulling is removed by polishing. Most polishing machines work on a similar principle to a friction huller, but instead of steel they have bronze bars, which do less damage to the beans. The bronze also gives the beans an attractive bluish hue. Beans milled by an impact huller are usually polished because they often look less tidy than friction-hulled beans.

Historically, polished beans were considered superior to unpolished ones, but there is, in fact, little difference in the resulting cup. The reverse snobbery, that polishing detracts from the cup by over-refining the bean, is sometimes voiced, but the evidence in the cup is doubtful.

GRADING AND SORTING

Green coffee beans, as they are now called, are graded first by size and then by density. With two exceptions, all coffee beans are of a fairly uniform size, and with the same proportions: they are flat on one side and half-oval on the other, and they are longer than they are wide. The exceptions are the peaberry, which is more oval in shape; and the elephant bean or *Maragogype*—a hybrid of arabica, which is naturally larger. Both of these bean types often command premium prices.

On the whole, the larger beans produce the better coffee. Size is expressed on a scale of 10 to 20, although some national quality grades are equivalent to size—Grade AA, for example. The beans are sized by being passed through a sieve, but at this stage even beans of the same size can have different weights, and damaged and shriveled beans must be removed.

The best way to separate the unwanted beans from the rest is to use gravity and air. The pneumatic method—a highly skilled process that is done by hand—uses an air jet to separate the heavy beans from the light beans. In an alternative method, gravimetric separators hold the beans on elevated trays and air is passed up and through them, causing the heavier beans to

Jute bags of coffee are loaded on to a ship, Colombia.

fall. This, too, is a highly skilled operation, and when it is carried out properly it enables more effective and uniform separation.

The next stage is to sort the beans to remove the ones with defects: stinkers, blacks, sours, foxes, and any over-fermented or unhulled beans. This is often done by eye—the beans are carried along a belt and the rejects are removed by hand.

Other methods include electronic color sorting, in which high-tech machinery uses light beams to detect defective beans. Increasingly sophisticated sorting machines are able to process beans much faster than any system involving the human eye, although there is still controversy in some quarters over which method produces the best result.

Different countries grade their beans according to different systems. The system used in Brazil, for instance, is complex but necessary. In general, however, there are six standard export grades; the top grade being SHB (strictly hard bean) or SHG (strictly high grown), which indicates that the beans were produced at a minimum altitude of 4,000 feet (1,200 meters) above sea level.

Grading coffee beans, Colombia.

All coffee is cupped—that is, tasted—before it is bought. The normal practice is that roasters buy the green beans from the country of production, perhaps directly from an exporter in that country or even from a large estate or co-operative that exports directly. This allows for greater control over the quality of the roast. Most roasters also make use of coffee importers, who bring green coffee into coffee-consuming countries in order to sell it to roasters.

These green coffee traders—including importers, brokers, agents, and dealers—normally have good contacts with sources of coffee in the producing countries. Some specialize in certain origins, or work for certain estates or only with specific types of coffee. Whatever they do, the traders play an important role in the coffee business, keeping the finance flowing from the roasters to the producing countries, and making sure a steady supply of coffee from the producing countries is available for roasters. The efficiency of this system is one reason why the coffee business represents the second most valuable trade on earth, after oil.

EXPORTING THE BEANS

Well over 6 million tons of green coffee are produced each year in origins all over the world. Most of this coffee will begin the journey from the plantations on a pack animal, but then its journey to the tables of the world will be by road, river, rail, sea and, in some cases, by air.

As we have seen, until it is ready to be sold and exported, the beans are kept and transported in their parchment shells. Although this increases the bulk and therefore the costs of storage and transportation, the parchment does protect the beans. Traditionally, almost all green beans are packed in coarse fiber bags made of jute or sisal, most of which hold 130 pounds (60 kilograms). The size of these bags varies between origins: in Hawaii, bags holding 100 pounds (45 kilograms) are common; while in Puerto Rico, the bags can hold as much as 200 pounds (90 kilograms). (A few origins make a point of shipping their green beans in an unusual and distinctive packaging; for example, Jamaica Blue Mountain's expensive and sought-after beans are always despatched in specially designed wooden barrels.)

After hulling, the bags are shipped from the origin port, in containers that hold around 250 standard bags, or sometimes on wooden pallets.

Increasingly, however, the traditional bags are being dispensed with altogether at the transport stage, in favor of shipping the coffee

Jamaican coffee is shoveled into a wooden barrel for transportation.

in bulk inside the containers. Once the inside of the container has been lined with what amounts to a huge plastic bag, it can be filled with loose beans—up to 22 tons of them in each container. When these containers reach their destination—the large roasting plants of North America or Europe, mainly—they can simply be upended into modern silo systems that are standard at all of the biggest coffee-roasting concerns.

Pests and humidity can cause real problems during transit, and the logistics companies (shipping lines and specialized warehousing firms) normally take measures to prevent them.

When it arrives at its destination, the coffee is either sent on to another warehouse to be stored or sent directly to the roaster.

THE WORLD'S BIGGEST COFFEE-PRODUCING COUNTRIES

1.	BRAZIL: 32.9 million bags	6.	ETHIOPIA: 4.5 million bags
2.	COLOMBIA: 11.9 million bags	7.	MEXICO: 4 million bags
3.	VIETNAM: 11 million bags	8.	GUATEMALA: 3.6 million bags
4.	INDONESIA: 6.7 million bags	9.	HONDURAS: 2.9 million bags
5.	INDIA: 4.6 million bags	10.	UGANDA: 2.7 million bags

(Production in the 2005/06 crop year, in standard 130lb (60kg) bags
—source: International Coffee Organization)

TRADE AND FAIR TRADE

It would be difficult to mention coffee and not talk about a relatively new phenomenon of the trade: "fairly traded" coffee, a term to which the traditional coffee traders originally objected, as it implied that all the rest of the trade was unfair. It is a matter of opinion whether this is the case, but the term "fair trade" has now come to stand for a method of ensuring that more of what the consumer pays for coffee reaches the farmer directly, with less being diverted to middlemen and traders between the consumer and the grower in the origin country.

The international trade in green (the raw and unroasted) coffee is based on the futures markets in New York (for arabica coffee) and London (for robusta). These markets, just like the stock market, respond to what is called "sentiment"—the way that traders feel about things like the weather and its effect on production, the availability of supply for the market, and which origin's coffees are needed and which are not. Just like the stock market, the futures market rises and falls, and the price traders and roasters are prepared to pay for green coffee is directly linked to it.

The coffee industry all over the world is reckoned to employ around 25 million people, the vast majority of which are small farmers in the origin countries producing the beans themselves. In the late 1990s, the markets responded to a glut of green coffee and prices fell to well below the cost of production in many origin countries. This situation, which lasted for several years until the start of the twenty-first century, was known as the coffee crisis, and caused hardship for many coffee producers and their families worldwide—especially those who could not easily switch into other crops.

The fair trade movement was not new at the time of the crisis, and it was not limited to coffee, but it was publicity about the coffee crisis that made it catch on with consumers. Several organizations—including the Fairtrade Foundation, Rainforest Alliance, and Utz Kapeh—came into their own during these tough times for coffee growers, allying with roasters with the aim of making sure that more of the revenues of coffee went to the farmers.

At first, smaller specialty roasters were the only ones that took part in these fair trade programs, but—as of 2006—virtually every large roaster is involved in some way in one of the programs; in some cases even devising schemes of their own. Under the schemes, roasters normally buy directly from an estate, a farmer, or a cooperative in the producing country, and then charge a slightly higher amount for the coffee at retail. The fair trade organization then ensures that a predetermined amount, which is well above the cost of production, is paid to the farmer, allowing him and his family to continue to produce coffee, while educating his children and looking after the environment.

A worker picks coffee cherries on a fair trade plantation in Costa Rica.

Most of the programs aim to make the coffee business sustainable for the growers and, if necessary, reduce their dependency on growing coffee. Often the schemes help to provide social programs for coffee communities and make sure that the environmental impact of coffee production is reduced as far as possible. Each of the programs certifies that the farm or cooperative involved comes up to a certain standard of social responsibility and care for the environment, in exchange for offering a guaranteed "fair" price for all the coffee bought from the farm or cooperative.

A number of roasters have gone one step further, with so-called "relationship" coffee—a system that links them directly with coffee-growing communities in origin. When a coffee-growing community agrees to supply coffee directly to a roaster at a certain quality for a guaranteed price (perhaps over several seasons), the roaster (and, by extension, the consumer that buys the final product) is linked to the coffee-growing community. The roaster could perhaps use the extra money produced by the premium on the retail price to provide school equipment, build a community center, or improve other facilities in the grower community. In this way, consumers can feel that they are directly helping the weakest part of the chain, which is at the producer end, and making a difference.

Critics of fair trade or "ethical" coffees say that they unfairly single out very few coffee producers for the treatment and prices that all growers should be getting. Nevertheless, its proponents say that, even in a limited way, fair trade is an example of the way the market could work, and there is little doubt that those farming communities involved in the programs are seeing significant benefits.

At present, these "ethical" coffees have more of a market share in Europe than they do in North America, but everywhere the demand for these has been growing significantly faster than for mainstream coffee.

ORGANIC AND TRACEABLE COFFEE

Probably the majority of the world's coffee is produced organically, without the use of chemical fertilizers and pesticides, but not for environmental reasons. Most small growers simply cannot afford to use these expensive inputs, and therefore rely on traditional methods of propagation and maintenance to give the best yield possible.

However, with increasing interest in organically grown produce in consuming countries, the demand for organic coffee has also been on the rise. The result is the advent of certified organic coffee, which has been audited throughout its production, and has been kept within its own channel and away from other coffee throughout the long journey from the farm to the cup. Inspectors not only check the production facilities in origin countries to make sure that the standard is being maintained, but

Organic coffee with the Fair Trade logo.

also examine warehouses and roasting plants in consuming nations to be certain that no non-organic coffee can make its way into the production chain at any point.

While the benefits of drinking organic coffee are debatable, two things are clear: consumers want it in increasing quantities, and are prepared to pay a premium to get it. In a perfect system, this would reward organic producers in the origin countries for their efforts at maintaining standards and keeping their production pure. Unfortunately, not all organic coffee, even if it is certified, is sold as such, because of the vagaries of the market and the fact that more organic coffee is grown than can yet be sold at a higher price. For example, all coffee from the Galapagos Islands is organic, but not certified as such—no fertilizers, pesticides, or other chemicals can be used on the island. Nevertheless, certified organic coffee—most of it from Latin America, and some of it also ethically traded—is getting a larger share of the overall business, and many roasters offer at least one organic coffee variety.

Virtually all certified coffee, be it organic, fairly traded, or sustainable, feeds into the current culture of identifying the source of food products, which has captured the imagination of consumers who would like to know the exact provenance of what they put on their tables. "Traceability" is the new buzzword in coffee, and it means being able to identify exactly the source of any consignment of coffee—often right down to the individual farm or estate in the origin country. More and more coffee packagers are taking this seriously, identifying the geographical region and the topography where the coffee was grown, and perhaps also adding a bit of history about the farm and the people that actually grew and processed the coffee at origin. Once again, this is a way of establishing a connection between consumers and the people in producing countries that grew the coffee that they are enjoying.

Costa Rican workers harvest coffee cherries by hand.

TASTING COFFEE

The founder of Seattle's Best Coffee, Jim Stewart, tastes coffee.

Different coffees come from all around the world and are prepared in a variety of ways, offering the drinker a huge choice of flavors and styles—ranging from light to full bodied, and from very acidic to lightly acidic. The sheer quantity of varieties can be rather overwhelming or confusing for a newcomer to gourmet or specialty coffees. However, just as there is a fairly well-defined and widely understood system for appraising wines, so there is a comparable system for coffee.

A professional taster (normally working for a green coffee trader or a coffee roaster) will have a selection of equipment, including a large number of white cups or, together with hundreds of sample boxes, trays for roasted and green coffee, scales for measuring, a small grinder, a small sample roaster, a spittoon, tasting spoons and, in the best-equipped and most up-to-date establishments, equipment for measuring the moisture content, the roast color, and even the chemical composition.

The appearance of beans varies to the trained eye. In terms of flavor, the coffee from different areas can be loosely classified. Coffee from South America has a bright acid and clean flavor; some East African, Yemeni, and Ethiopian coffees taste winy; arabicas from Indonesia are heavier bodied; while Indian coffees are less acid but can be equally full bodied.

When a coffee is being appraised, the taster has 10 criteria to consider:

TYPE: e.g., washed robusta, unwashed arabica
TASTE: e.g., strictly soft, harsh
BODY: e.g., lacking, too heavy
ACIDITY: e.g., some, too much at the top
AGE: old to fresh
DEFECTS: e.g., sour, grassy, musty
CUP: e.g., roast, watery, burnt, old
OVERALL ASSESSMENT: e.g., neutral, spicy, hard
AROMA: weak to strong
FULLNESS: slight to considerable

To become a good coffee cupper, as a taster is called in the trade, takes many years' experience, which is usually gained on the job. Tasting coffee is similar to tasting tea or wine, although it is agreed that wine is easier to taste because it persists on the palate for longer.

The coffee taster first assesses the green beans, noting their appearance and aroma, and checking for visual defects. Next, after roasting in small sample roasters, he or she smells a freshly roasted and ground sample. Using several cups for each coffee sample, the taster infuses the samples in near-boiling water, and then noses the brew. After 3 minutes, the brew is lightly stirred and smelled again. The resulting foam and floating grounds are removed and the tasting proper begins. The taster takes a spoonful of coffee into his or her mouth with a vigorous (and noisy!) slurping action that aerates the coffee and enhances tasting. The taster then "chews" it around the mouth,

COFFEE TASTERS' VOCABULARY

Professional tasters use a variety of scales and notes to describe and assess the brews they taste. Here are just a few of the ways they describe the various aspects they are looking for in each cup:

AROMA: animal-like, ashy, burnt/smoky, chemical/medical, chocolaty, caramel/malty, earthy, floral, fruity, grainy/green/herbal, nutty, rancid/rotten, rubber-like, spicy, tobacco-like, winy, woody.

TASTE: acid, bitter, salty, sour, sweet.

MOUTHFEEL: balance of flavors, astringency, body.

Robusta is often mustier and has a more burnt flavor, while arabica is more citrus with higher acidity.

Professional cupping session at Mercanta, Kingston-upon-Thames, England.

ensuring that all the taste receptors on the tongue are covered. The coffee also has to be lifted to the back of the mouth, where flavor retention or aftertaste can be detected; this is a major indication of the coffee's body. The taster then spits out the sample before repeating the procedure with all the samples, taking notes as each brew is sampled. Many tasters use a one to five or even a one to ten scale, although others use more individual methods.

Do not be deterred from attempting your own coffee tasting. You will be surprised at how quickly you learn to differentiate between varieties in order to recognize your favorites. Eventually, you will also be able to ask for, and even create, interesting and rewarding blends.

The first step, as in wine tasting, is to acquire the correct vocabulary and to gain experience in using it. There is no substitute for drinking different kinds of coffee as often as possible. This will give you an opportunity to find out which kinds are available and which kinds you like—or do not like.

TASTING COFFEE

Assemble green beans, grind, and spoon as shown.

Pour near-boiling water
on to the grinds.

Nose coffee, then break crust of
grind that has formed.

Nose coffee again, then "suck" a spoonful into your mouth.

TASTING COFFEES AT HOME

Invite two friends to taste three different coffees. For your first tasting do not look for fine differences, but think about identifying the main characteristics of, say, an East African and an Asian coffee. For example, Ethiopian coffee is high in acidity and low in body, while a Sumatran coffee will have a low acidity and a full body.

You will need three sets of three cups—white, medium-sized ones are best—and, if you want to spit out the coffee as the professionals do, a spittoon.

Grind a tablespoon of beans for each taster and put the grinds in the bottom of a cup. Professional tasters measure the amount very precisely: some use scales to measure out $^1/_3$ ounce (10 grams); others prefer just under $^1/_2$ ounce (12 grams). Write the name of the coffee on a piece of paper and place it under the cup. After grinding one type of bean, shake or brush away as much as possible of the detritus before you grind the next. Professionals even grind a small amount of the next beans between batches to make sure that none of the previous type is left. You should grind sufficient beans to allow for a small amount of ground coffee to be presented in a dish near to the tasting sample.

Incidentally, the grinder must be a good one and be able to produce a consistent grind. You are looking for a grinding that will provide grounds of 0.2 to 0.6 millimeter with 7 to 8 percent powder. The grind you need is that which is suitable for a drip (filter) machine, because this will release the aroma over the optimum period. Too fine, and the aroma will be released too soon; too coarse, and insufficient aroma will be released.

The amount of water is also precisely measured, because too much will make the coffee watery, while too little will make it harsh. Draw the water freshly from a cold tap, allowing the tap to run for a few seconds before you fill the kettle or pot. Switch off the kettle just before it boils, and pour the water on to the ground beans. If you have $^1/_3$ ounce (10 grams) of coffee in an average-sized cup, you need to fill the cup to just below the rim. Make sure that the water is equally hot for each cup, bringing it back to near-boiling point for each one if necessary. If you live in an area that has very hard water, you may need to boil it first to remove some of the chalk, which can affect the flavor. Some tasters prefer to make coffee in a pot and pour it into the tasting cups, but most pour the water directly on to the ground coffee in individual cups.

Although the technical word for tasting coffee is "cupping," many tasters say that clear glasses are better. These make it possible to inspect the brew more closely. If you decide to use glasses, choose ones that are wider at the rim than wine glasses (which should be wider in the center than at the top). The wider glasses make it easier to appreciate the aroma.

The taster noses the fresh ground coffee, then the cup or glass into which the water has been poured. At this stage the brew is not stirred. After 2 to 3 minutes nose the coffee again, using a silver-plated spoon (a soup spoon is ideal) to break the crust of grinds that will

Two of the best coffees from Kenya, AA (top) and Peaberry (bottom).

When you are tasting, try to be precise and to use professional terminology.

have formed on the surface. This will give you your first impression of the coffee.

Take a couple of sniffs. Remember that our olfactory sense diminishes after only 2 to 4 seconds' exposure to a smell, which is our body's way of dealing with all the new smells it picks up throughout the day. If it did not and the old smells were retained in our consciousness, they would mingle with the new. Some tasters try nosing with alternate nostrils, but usually a few seconds' break is sufficient to revive your sense of smell. Write down your first impressions. Was the coffee earthy, ashy, floral—or something else altogether? Repeat this exercise with all the coffees you are tasting—and do not forget to rinse your spoon in clean water between coffees.

Next, gently stir the brew and take up a spoonful. Suck this into your mouth, slurping rather than drinking. You may think that this looks (and sounds) inelegant, and it does. But you are all doing this, so there is no need to stand on ceremony or to be shy. "Chew" the coffee around your mouth to get some idea of the acidity and body. Make sure you lift the coffee to the back of your mouth, so that you can detect aftertaste and flavor retention. This is a good measure of body, because the more

aftertaste is present, the more body the coffee is said to have. The sense of body is an important one: is the coffee full bodied or not? Acidity is more difficult to define, but you will feel it on the edge of your tongue. Spit out the coffee and write down your impressions.

Views differ on the second tasting. Many people feel that tea and coffee are harder to taste than wine because the alcohol in wine encourages persistence on the palate and helps to create an identity. Some tasters find it difficult to measure the range of variables in tea and coffee with one or even two tastings. You might, therefore, want to try all the coffees being tasted, "chewing" them to measure the body and acidity, and then to taste them again, but more aggressively. This time you are looking for individual characteristics and flavors—is it sweet or salty, is there a flavor of charcoal, or is it musty? To taste properly you must "slurp" as hard as you can, drawing the coffee into the back of the mouth and spraying the soft palate. You will probably be making a lot of noise and quite a mess, but it should be fun, too. Remember to make a note of your impressions.

After 15 minutes, by which time the brews will have cooled, taste them again.

BLIND TASTING

After a blind tasting of six different coffees—from Brazil, Cameroon (robusta), Colombia, Costa Rica, Ivory Coast (robusta), and Kenya—among a group of French consumers, the International Coffee Organization found that:

Colombian coffee was rated as having the strongest aroma; it was rated significantly higher than Costa Rican, Cameroonian, Brazilian, and Kenyan. Only coffee from the Ivory Coast was higher for some tasters.

Acidity was a difficult characteristic for the tasters to assess. Costa Rican and Colombian coffees were found to have the most acidity. Very dark-roast coffees tend to lose almost all their acidity, unlike light-roast coffees, which develop high acidity.

Kenyan coffee was perceived to be significantly less bitter than Colombian, Costa Rican, and Brazilian coffees, although the latter were dark roasted and somewhat bitter, but no less bitter than the two robusta coffees. (A dark roast increases bitterness more in arabica than in robusta coffee, but Kenyan beans are the exception that proves this general rule.)

A fruity flavor, which might be expected to disappear with a very dark roast, was still identified by the tasters, and Kenyan coffee was perceived as being markedly more fruity than the two robustas, but not significantly more fruity than the Brazilian, Colombian, and Costa Rican coffees.

When the tasters were asked to identify burnt flavors, the results were similar to the tasting for bitterness. The participants could be divided into two groups—those who could distinguish the burnt characteristics and those who could not. Both Costa Rican and Colombian coffees were, however, perceived as having a noticeably greater degree of burnt aroma, or flavor, than the Kenyan coffee.

When it came to assessing body, Costa Rican coffee was found to be the most full bodied—the difference was most notable when the coffee was compared with the coffees from Kenya, Brazil, Ivory Coast, and Cameroon, although it was less marked when compared with Colombian coffee.

On average, all the coffees were regarded as having an aftertaste of medium intensity, with the Costa Rican coffee scoring significantly higher than all three of the coffees from Africa.

In general, the tasters expressed a preference for Kenyan coffee over those from Brazil, Colombia, and Ivory Coast, with the other two coffees coming second after the Kenyan coffee.

This tasting shows that, at least among this group of French consumers, the preferred coffee was the one that had the lowest intensities of aroma and bitterness, the lowest intensity of burnt and full-bodied characteristics, and a high degree of fruitiness. Colombian coffee, which has markedly different characteristics to Kenyan coffee, was significantly less liked than the African bean, and although the robusta from Cameroon was very close in perception to the Kenyan coffee, it was perceived as being more bitter and definitely less fruity.

ROASTING COFFEE

After roasting, the beans must be moved around the pan so that they cool evenly.

When it is done well, roasting coffee beans is an art. The process creates flavor and aroma; without it, none of the flavor of coffee is apparent in the cup. Green beans are relatively stable and, if stored correctly, will last for years.

During roasting, the heat causes a series of chemical reactions to take place. Starches are converted into sugars, which caramelize, some types of acids are created and others are broken down. The basic cellular structure of the bean eventually breaks down, causing the bean to "pop," just like popcorn. Proteins are broken down into peptides, and these emerge through the surface of the bean in the form of oils. Moisture and carbon dioxide are burnt off and, in a darker roast, pure carbon is created.

The aromatic oils are really at the heart of roasting. They are called coffee essence, coffee oil or, more accurately, caffeol. These aromatic oils are volatile—that is, they are the elements that carry the flavors and aromas—and they are water soluble, which means that those flavors

and aromas can be enjoyed in the cup. The great enemy of roasted beans is oxygen, for as soon as beans are roasted they begin to lose the flavors that have been brought to the surface by roasting. The oils that have been precipitated to the surface are oxidized and in a very short time they produce a sooty, rancid flavor.

The roaster himself can cause untold damage. If the beans have not been roasted at the necessary temperature—usually around 464°F (240°C)—for the correct amount of time, according to the required roasting result, the oils will not have been brought out to the surface, and the flavor will be underdeveloped. If the roasting is done at too high a temperature or for too long, the beans will taste thin and burnt. Burnt coffee is exceedingly unpleasant.

Most roasting machines are gas-fired. They work at temperatures of around 550°F (290°C), and for the first 5 minutes or so the high temperature burns off any free moisture. Thereafter, the residual moisture is forced from

Professional roasting machine, Switzerland.

the beans (this causes the cracking or popping sound). Next, when the beans reach a temperature of about 400°F (200°C), they start to turn a darker brown, and it is at this point that the oils start to emerge. This process is called pyrolysis. From this point the person who is roasting has to begin to make crucial decisions, for if the beans are left for too long, they will be ruined.

Some larger machines, of the kind that are found in commercial roasters, move the beans along a screw inside the drum, and when they reach the end of the screw, they are done. Such expensive machines are viable only when large quantities of beans are being roasted. A local specialty roaster will probably use what is known as a "batch" roaster, which is basically a drum, rotating horizontally, with a fire beneath and a fan to draw away the smoke and fumes. An alternative method is more indirect, heating air and then using that to move and roast the coffee at the same time. Pressurized roasting works very quickly with this hot air method and roasts can be achieved in 3 to 5 minutes. Modern environmental regulations imposed by

ROASTER'S VOCABULARY

Here are just some of the words used to describe the same roast. Ask your coffee merchant to explain so you can describe precisely what you want.

LIGHT ROAST: half city, cinnamon, New England, light

MEDIUM: American, medium/high, breakfast, regular

FULL MEDIUM: light French, Viennese, city, full city

DARK/HIGH ROAST: New Orleans, European, French, after dinner, Italian

VERY DARK ROAST (SHINY, OILY APPEARANCE): Continental, dark French, heavy

local authorities insist that roasting is clean from smoke and smell, so various methods of afterburning are put into practice.

Simple batch roasting relies on the skill of the roaster to judge the correct color. With modern computer technology, the moisture content of the green bean is measured and programmed "profile" roasting will assure the exact color on every roast.

A smaller roaster or retailer will probably use an 11 pound (5 kilogram) machine, while a serious amateur or a retailer who is very concerned about freshness might prefer one of the tabletop roasters that are now available for enthusiasts.

Some typical roasts (from left): unroasted, medium roast, medium to full roast, high roast, Continental roast, French roast, and unroasted.

It is important that the beans are kept moving during the roasting process, not only to ensure that the batch roasts evenly but also to stop them from burning, which could cause them to catch fire.

When the beans are taken from the roaster, they are cooled, preferably by air, but sometimes in water. The more quickly and completely the cooling is done the better, because roasted beans will continue to cook as they cool down.

The only universal terminology among coffee roasters are the words "low," "medium," and "high" or, sometimes, "light," "medium," and "dark," and these words mean different things to different people. In the United States, the vocabulary is broader, with expressions such as "full city roast," which usually means that the beans have been taken to the stage just before they would become "high," "dark," or "European." In the first decade of the twenty-first century, with the advent of the specialty coffee sector and the spread of the coffee house chains which often favor them, darker roasts have become more common, and it appears that many consumers prefer them.

There is no reason why you cannot mix light- with dark-roast beans if that is what you want.

However, you should bear in mind that some roasts are not appropriate for some coffees, just as some coffees are more appropriate for different times of day.

It would, for example, be a waste to high roast an Ethiopian bean, because you would lose the individual character of the coffee. It would also be a sin to dark roast Yauco Selecto or Kona beans, because you would lose the classic flavor you bought them for. Other quality gourmet beans will, on the other hand, gain something new and interesting from dark roasting. Some Mexican beans, for example, become interestingly sweet when they are dark roasted.

Some coffees, such as Guatemalan Antigua, will retain their acidity and fruit when they are high roasted. Other coffees are more difficult: for instance, Kenyan coffee should not be high roasted, because its natural high acidity will spoil the distinctive Kenyan flavor; Sumatran coffees, as another example, usually have a very full body but low to medium acidity, and at a higher roast they do lose their acidity but tend to acquire a rather syrupy body.

In general, darker roasts mean that less of the true character of the bean will be apparent and bitterness will dominate the overall flavor.

Freshly roasted beans in the cooling pan.

ROASTING BEANS AT HOME

The most difficult coffee-related activity is to roast your own beans at home. However, the freshness of the roasted coffee is the first essential when it comes to brewing quality coffee, and probably we have all bought stale coffee from a retailer, even if only once. There is absolutely nothing to compare with the taste of beans you have roasted, then ground and made into coffee in your own kitchen. So, it is worth the effort. (It can be difficult to obtain small quantities of green beans for home roasting, but specialty coffee roasters often have a fine selection available.)

The cheapest way is to roast the beans in the oven. This has the benefit of allowing you to control the temperature so that your home is not completely taken over by the smell of roasting coffee. Preheat your oven to 450°F (230°C / gas mark 8). Remember that air must be allowed to move under and among the beans, so they must not be spread too thickly. Leave the beans in the oven for about 10 minutes and watch for the color change. Listen for the sounds of the beans cracking, and keep checking the color. When the beans are just a little lighter than you want, take them out of the oven and allow them to cool. The beans will continue to cook internally for another 2 to 4 minutes. (Coffee roasting often produces a lot of smoke, so be prepared for this if you want to use the oven roasting method. You will also find an oven thermometer invaluable.)

You can also buy stove-top home roasters, but the best kind are the traditional roaster pan or hot air, popcorn popper types. These either have a handle that drives two vertical plates inside the body or an electric motor that moves the plates, rotating the beans as they roast. The hot air types are easier to use, as the timing mechanism controls the roasting time and the roast color. You might be able to find one in a good hardware store or on the Internet. Hottop, Hearthware I-Roast, and Swissmar Bravi all supply notable home roasting machines.

When the beans are ready, take them from the roaster or oven, place them in an ovenproof bowl, and put the bowl near a window, or even outdoors, to cool.

Hottop home coffee roaster.

GRINDING COFFEE

Early twentieth-century table-fitted grinder, made from solid metal.

Whenever coffee is processed, its effective life, in terms of flavor, is shortened. Green beans, as we have noted, can last for years, but after roasting (unless the beans are packaged immediately) there is only a week of full flavor and, at best, two weeks of reduced flavor. After grinding, the coffee's life is reduced to a few days at the most.

In any good coffee shop, when you choose the origin or blend of beans you want, you will probably be asked if you need the beans to be ground. If you do want them ground, make sure that you specify the method you will be using to brew the coffee, because this will affect the grind. The objective, of course, is to get the most flavor from the beans. Generally, the rule of thumb is the faster the infusion, the finer the grind required.

The basic categories of grind are "coarse," "medium," and "fine." The finer grinds do not need to remain in contact with water for as long as the coarser grinds. The coarsest grind, therefore, is used in the classic jug method. The French press / plunger / cafetière and drip / filter methods require coarser grinds than espresso. This principle indicates that espresso requires a very fine grind, as the water is only in contact with the coffee for about 20 seconds. The exception to this rule is Turkish ground coffee, which is actually heated in the pan to create a very strong and bitter drink.

The finer / faster rule should only be used as a guide. For example, if you try to use an espresso grind in your filter machine, you may find that the water takes longer to filter through and the flavor is not improved. If you want to make a stronger or weaker brew, it is much better simply to increase or reduce the proportion of ground coffee to water rather than to vary the grind.

TYPES OF GRIND

Very fine grind (espresso).

Fine grind (filter).

Medium grind (all purpose, filter, or French press/cafetière).

Medium coarse grind (French press/cafetière).

Coarse grind (percolator or jug method).

Pulverized (Turkish).

GRINDING AT HOME

Basic wooden box grinder with a drawer to catch the ground coffee.

It cannot be said too often that the best thing of all is to roast, grind, and brew coffee on the spot. (This is the traditional method in Ethiopia, the homeland of arabica.) However, even if we had all the equipment, most of us would be content with grinding beans just before we prepare the brew. The difference between freshly ground coffee beans and beans that were ground only a few days before is huge. Most of the experts consider grinding to be the most important part of the coffee preparation process. Without good grinding, you cannot produce a good cup of coffee—it is as simple as that.

Grinding your own beans is easy to do. There are lots of different coffee grinders on the market; they are not too frightening to buy and they take up little room in the kitchen.

The oldest way to reduce beans to a brewable form is by mortar and pestle. This method is not quick and the results are not consistent, producing grounds that are suitable only for longer infusion methods or for Turkish coffee.

The second oldest method is probably the millstone—and this is possibly the best, although probably far from the most practical for most consumers. This type of grinder originated in the Middle East and is a handheld cylinder, containing the equivalent of two millstones in the form of two corrugated steel disks, which crush the beans.

Next comes the wooden box grinder. You put the beans in the top and, after grinding, pull them out in the little drawer at the bottom. It is worth paying extra to get the best possible quality—Zassenhaus is a brand of wooden box grinder that is often recommended. Cheaper versions will not last as long, nor will they produce a fine, consistent grind. These machines can also be used when traveling, as they are much more portable than a standard electric machine, and do not rely on the vagaries of currents and plug adapters. However, it can be difficult to vary the grind for different coffee preparations using this type of equipment.

The fourth main type is the old-fashioned, wall-mounted or table-fitted type of grinder or mincer. These are good, solid metal objects. If you appreciate antiques, you may still be able to find these available on the Internet, although they have long ago been superseded by modern, electric machines.

The main group consists of electric, motor-driven machines, which can either have blades or two crushing burr plates. Burrs (see page 44) are much to be preferred. The very top of the range is a professional machine, such as the Mahlkönig Guatemala, which can be used at home as well, if cost is no object. The Gaggia MDF has 36 different grind settings, and the great advantage of this kind of grinder is that you can get the exact quantity with just the degree of grind that you want. The Rancilio Rocky is a medium-priced machine that can double as a commercial grinder, and the Capresso Infinity is thought to be the best entry-level grinder for espresso. A number of other small espresso grinders that will measure the precise quantity required for one shot of espresso—approximately $1/4$ ounce (7 grams)—are also available for domestic use.

With a cheaper grinder, you need to measure out the precise number of beans and then grind for varying lengths of time to get the kind of grind you require. If you drink espresso (and make it yourself at home), you will need one of the more expensive machines, because a blade grinder simply will not produce the consistently fine grind that is essential.

Experience with your chosen grinder is the best way to work out the grinding time required to make the best cup of coffee by the method you prefer.

Bunn's electric coffee grinder.

BLADES VS BURRS

There can be no doubt that burrs give a much better grind than a blade. A blade does not so much mill or grind the beans; it slashes them—first to ribbons, and then to irregular pieces. There will be a fine powder around the edge, and chunks of bean at the center.

Nevertheless, even freshly "slashed" beans still have much more flavor than ground coffee that has been stored for any length of time, and the blade grinders do have one advantage over the burr grinders—they are much cheaper. A standard blade grinder retails for around one-fifth of the price of the Gaggia MDF, and a basic burr grinder is normally at least twice as expensive as a blade grinder. Nevertheless, if you have the opportunity to compare the flavors resulting from the two grinding methods, you may be surprised at the extra edge of quality that results from the even grind produced by burrs. A good burr grinder will cost more than $100; beware of the cheaper burr grinders, especially if you like to make espresso at home, because they probably are not up to the job.

Ideally (if you do not have a small box grinder), keep your old electric handheld or other blade grinder for holidays, second homes, extensive traveling, and so on. If you must use this type, do not hold your finger on the button for a long time. Grind in short pulses of 2 to 5 seconds, which prevents the beans from heating up too much, and give the grinder a gentle shake or tap it on the table to move the contents around between pulses.

Gaggia MDF domestic coffee grinder.

MAKING COFFEE

Barista Luigi Lupi makes the perfect cappuccino.

Perhaps one of the reasons that the drinking and enjoyment of coffee has spread so widely around the world is that it lends itself so well to so many different ways of preparation, and satisfies so many different palates. Nevertheless, the basic principle is universal and common to all methods of making coffee: the ground beans are soaked in hot water to extract a liquor with flavor and aroma.

Although the coffee bean came to us from Arabia, the Arabian way of making coffee did not spread, and even though there are now dozens of ways to make coffee, there is still a fundamental difference between all of these methods and the traditional Arabian way, in which coffee is boiled three times. Boiling coffee is bad, because it boils off the caffeol, flavors, and aromas, and it exaggerates the bitter-tasting elements in the infusion. To overcome this, the Arabs added cardamom to their coffee. We tend to look to machinery and technology to prevent the problem in the first place.

There is no one "best" method of making coffee. The "best" method is the one that suits you, and you have to consider your own convenience and preferences and the time the different methods take. There is also, of course, the indefinable element of the ritual involved in making coffee. As a break during a busy day or after a stressful time in the office, it can be fun to take the time to make a really good cup of coffee—just for you.

Various coffee-making accoutrements.

TURKISH COFFEE

The coffee that we call Turkish is, perhaps, made in the same way as the earliest coffee drinkers used to brew their beans. Very finely ground coffee, sugar, and water are put—in that order—into a small brass jug with a long handle, called an *ibriq*. You should use two level teaspoons of coffee for each cup and add one teaspoon of sugar for each teaspoon of coffee. When the brew has boiled, take it off the heat. As it boils, the liquid rises up the neck of the *ibriq*, so make sure that you do not fill it to the brim. The brew is brought to the boil three times in all before being served. Traditionally, cardamom is added to this kind of coffee. You can buy and grind your own (but do not use your coffee grinder for the cardamom seeds), and you will need one seed for each cup.

It has to be said that this is not the ideal way to treat good coffee, but it is an interesting drink and has an individual taste.

PERCOLATOR

The percolator was invented in 1827 in France and soon became very popular in the United States. It does produce a wonderful aroma in the home and a satisfying sound as the water gurgles through and around the system. That said, percolators boil coffee and produce a bitter-tasting brew; most have now been superseded by other methods.

American Universal percolator from the 1880s.

CONA VACUUM

The vacuum method of making coffee was devised in 1840 by Robert Napier, a Scottish marine engineer. It works on the principle of a globe, half-filled with water, being placed over a heat source with dry coffee in a receiver above. When it is stable, the heat source is removed and the coffee enters the globe by means of a siphon between the two. This was later marketed under the Cona brand name.

You may sometimes see these machines in old-fashioned restaurants, and you may even come across one in a second-hand shop (although the glass globes are fragile and easily cracked). There is something rather alchemical about the method, and it is an interesting way of making coffee that can be excellent if you take care not to let the coffee itself boil. They are, however, not convenient for everyday use.

An original Cona balloon, once a popular method of brewing coffee.

THE DRIP METHOD

The drip or filter method is the most popular system in the West today, and was invented by a Frenchman, M. de Belloy.

The unit is in two halves. The hot water is poured over coarsely ground coffee, which is held in a paper filter in the upper section. The brew drips down, by gravity, through the filter into the pouring pot below. This takes between 6 and 8 minutes and the result is a clear drink that contains few grounds.

Electric versions of this method, known as filter machines, are able to produce the correct amount of water at the optimum temperature for making the most of the beans before it passes through a permanent or paper filter. One of the advantages of a paper filter is the convenience—you simply throw it away after use. Paper also provides a more comprehensive

Drip filter machine, from Bunn.

Technivorm's Moccamaster filter machine.

filtration material than the permanent filters in some machines.

There are several styles, makes, and additional features available, although none of them seems to have much effect on the final cup. Of the permanent filters, the best are the "gold" ones, which allow more sediment elements into the coffee and thereby give it a different texture. These machines require a slightly coarser grind.

The correct hand-drip method is to draw cold water and bring it almost to the boil. Having warmed the pot, pour some water into the ground coffee to initiate some caffeol activity, then pour in the required amount of water.

The range of filter machines available is large, but the most recommended are Bunn's domestic range, KitchenAid Proline, Technivorm, or Fetco's Extractor series.

FRENCH PRESS OR CAFETIÈRE

The plunger pot system is a simple way to make coffee.

Known as the French press in the United States and the cafetière in Europe, the plunger pot system is an excellent way to make coffee. Many people prefer coffee made this way because it extracts the full flavor from the ground beans, while other methods tend to remove some of the flavor; and paper filters can even add a taste of their own. The plunger pot is said to have been invented in 1933 by an Italian called Caliman who sold his design and patent to a Swiss national in order to escape from Italy during World War II.

The method could not be simpler. Warm the pot, put in the coarsely ground coffee (about ¹/₆ ounce [5 grams] for each cup), add the hot water, stir, and allow to steep for 4 to 5 minutes. Then push down the plunger—a stainless steel mesh—to separate the grounds from the liquid before serving the coffee direct from the press, which looks attractive on the table.

This is a convenient method, because the grounds are so easily disposed of, and it is possible to enjoy the full flavor of the coffee. There is also the advantage that you can buy different sizes of pot, so you can make the right amount of coffee to suit your needs. The only drawback is that if you make a brew for, say, after dinner, it will get cold quickly when it is left standing on the table. You can buy ceramic or even thermos-type presses, or you could use one of the "coffee cosies" now on the market. Alternatively, just make a fresh pot of coffee.

The Danish company Bodum makes the best of the less expensive presses. Nissan makes a recommended stainless steel version, which is more portable and therefore suitable for travel. The main thing to remember when you are choosing a French press or plunger pot is not to buy one with a nylon mesh. A stainless steel mesh is much better and will last far longer.

OPEN POT OR JUG

This, the most basic of methods, is, some believe, still the best way to make coffee. You will need very coarse grounds, which are placed in the bottom of the jug. Pour on the water, stir, allow it to steep for a few minutes, and pour, using a strainer to remove any grounds. Tradition says that an eggshell placed in the pot will absorb some of the sediment.

Danish Shelton stainless steel coffee pot by Arne Jacobsen, 1970s.

Stove-top espresso pot, the most popular way of making coffee in Italy.

ESPRESSO, MOCHA, AND NAPOLETANA

These three words—espresso, mocha, and napoletana—all describe those neat little stovetop makers of very dark coffee that seem to exist in every Italian kitchen. They have two chambers, and the water, which is in the lower one, is forced through the coffee and into the top chamber, from where it is poured. This method has few of the benefits of the plunger pot or filter method, although the little pots are undeniably attractive.

ESPRESSO AND CAPPUCCINO

Whatever else is uncertain about coffee—its origins, the most flavorful beans, the best way of brewing—you can be sure of one thing: whenever two or more serious coffee drinkers get together, they will discuss the finer points of making espresso and cappuccino.

Espresso is a brewing process by which the classic, dark-roasted cup of black coffee—full bodied but aromatic—is made, and it is possibly the most difficult and potentially the most expensive way to make coffee. Some say that the word espresso derives from the French word *exprès*, meaning "especially for" or "purposely for"—identifying the way that the drink is made especially for one person—but other sources suggest that the name comes from the Italian verb meaning "to put under pressure," which is exactly how the beverage is made. Boiling water and steam are forced through very finely ground coffee—preferably one without too much acidity, so Kenyan is not ideal—to produce a unique

La Pavoni Professional copper and brass espresso maker.

style of coffee with bite and great persistence on the palate. It is not just the rich, sweet flavor that makes espresso such a wonderful drink; when it is good it has an indefinable tang, a quality that fills the palate.

Authentic espresso accounts for only 10 percent of Italian coffee, although it is, literally, the basis of the other 90 percent, which comprises cappuccino, latte, and the other espresso-based beverages—most of which are made up of espresso and milk in various forms. Ideally, the most popular espresso drink, cappuccino, is one-third espresso, one-third milk and one-third froth. (One sign of consumer demand for cappuccino is the presence on supermarket shelves of instant cappuccino, a product that has been a great success for the instant coffee suppliers, at the same time as their main instant coffee varieties have shown little growth in most mature markets.)

Indifferent cappuccino is universally available, which is perhaps an indication that it is easier to make a cup that tastes pleasant enough than it is to produce good espresso. Really good cappuccino is, however, even more difficult to make than espresso. Every cup must be freshly made by a method that gets the best from the coffee. Unlike espresso, a little acidity is desirable in cappuccino (and Kenyan coffee can be used), but the real difficulty lies in preparing the milk, which must not be allowed to boil or its chemical character will alter and affect the overall flavor. (Some people do not like chocolate sprinkled on top of their cappuccino, but it does stop a skin forming if the milk has been allowed to boil.)

There are two main types of espresso machines available: old-fashioned piston-operated machines and electric semi- or fully automatic machines.

Piston-operated machines have a spring-loaded system that forces the water through the

Home espresso machine, by Briel.

coffee. These piston-handled machines look wonderful and, in the hands of a skilled barista, they produce excellent coffee. They are not ideal for less-experienced operators, however, and more and more people are turning to the semi- or fully automated machines that make it possible simply to flip a switch and wait until the cup is ready in a few seconds' time. These days, the only skill with these home units seems to lie in getting the milk for cappuccino to froth, which takes time and practice—although now even this can be handled completely automatically.

These electric espresso machines are easier to operate and more practical. Again, if you are thinking of purchasing such a unit, it is no good trying to economize. The cheaper models (under $100) that are available have no pump and therefore do not generate the required pressure to make real espresso. Even the cheaper pump machines (under $200) often have no boiler, which means that it is difficult to froth milk for a cappuccino or latte.

As a basic pump and boiler machine, Saeco's Aroma is recommended, as is the Solis SL line. The Rancilio Silvia is probably the most popular home espresso machine, but also highly rated (and expensive) are the home espresso machines from La Marzocco and Della Corte.

Many of these manufacturers supply grinders to go with their espresso machines. These sets are not cheap, but think how much you spend every morning if you stop and have a couple of espressos in a café on your way to work!

Professional café espresso maker from La Pavoni, 1930s.

MAKING ESPRESSO

Making good espresso at home is one of life's little challenges. It is worth remembering that often the more you are prepared to spend on a machine, the better the coffee will be. However, making good espresso should be regarded as a hobby—not as a lifetime's search for perfection. Professional baristas (the expert coffee bartenders you see in the best cafés) practice for years to achieve the perfect espresso and cappuccino, culminating perhaps in a chance to vie for the ultimate prize at the World Barista Championship, the "Olympics" of coffee, which takes place every year.

If you are not quite at this level, there are a few basic steps to follow on your way to a good espresso beverage. First, select the coffee. Almost any specialty coffee store will sell an espresso blend (some of which are entirely based on arabica beans), although there is no such thing as a specific espresso bean or roast. Some of the best espresso producers insist that some robusta in the blend is crucial to the flavor

MAKING ESPRESSO

A tamper is used to pack down the ground coffee in the filter basket.

The best coffee comes out first—black, then the crema.

Switch off before the coffee becomes bitter and watery.

Good, evenly
colored crema.

Thin crema, from
over-extraction.

Light tamping can
cause light crema.

and to the formation of the all-important *crema*. At any rate, because the process of making espresso tends to intensify the characteristics of whatever bean you select, you will probably want to use a blend. You might want to begin with a combination of an aromatic and fairly acidic Central American bean and a rich, full-bodied Indonesian bean.

Next, grind the beans. They should be finely ground, but not pulverized, as they would be for Turkish coffee. The grind is crucial: if it is too coarse, the brew will gush out thin and watery, not having extracted enough of the coffee, but if it is too fine, the coffee will become an over-extracted sludge that will block the filter, causing the brew to drip out too slowly and taste bitter. Most domestic machines come with a measuring scoop; you will need about $1/4$ ounce (7 grams) of coffee.

After grinding, the coffee must be tamped into the filter. The tamped ground coffee must not be so loose that the water flows straight through, but neither must it be tamped so tightly that nothing can get through. In a good machine, you will need quite firmly and vigorously to tamp the grounds down in the *gruppa* (the "group" or portable, removable filter head that holds the coffee on standard semi-automatic espresso machines). At first you may find it helpful to examine a just-used *gruppa* to check that you are tamping correctly.

When the coffee begins to come out from the nozzles, remember that the best comes first—the black, first extraction of the coffee which forms the main part of the espresso, followed by the caramel-colored *crema*. Switch off the machine after a few seconds of *crema*, because if you leave the machine on for too long, the coffee will be bitter and watery.

The vital indication of whether a cup of espresso is a good one is the presence of *crema*. As the coffee is discharged into the cup it should be covered with a caramel-colored layer, the *crema*, which is created by the oils in the coffee mixing with water and air during the extraction process. The *crema* should be evenly colored and as much as $1/4$ inch (5 millimeters) thick. As you drink, it should coat the side of the cup, like syrup. A dark-brown *crema* with a white dot or black hole in the middle is a sign that the espresso has been over-extracted and that it will taste harsh and bitter. A light-colored *crema*, on the other hand, indicates an under-extracted espresso that will taste weak.

The kind of coffee you use is a matter of personal preference. Traditionally, the character of espresso demands a high-roast bean, although a medium-roast coffee can do just as well. Until you get used to your machine, try richer, sweeter, dark-roast beans for espresso.

By the way, did you know that a standard shot of espresso has slightly less caffeine content than a mug of regular-brewed coffee? Dark roasts are thought to have slightly less caffeine as well, because the longer roasting process destroys more of the caffeine.

MAKING CAPPUCCINO

Once the fresh espresso is in the cup, you can begin to prepare the milk. You should always try to use semi-skimmed homogenized, because full-fat milk will mask the flavor of the coffee; and although some cafés use milk that is warm or at least at room temperature (because it does not take as long to foam as cold milk), you should use cold milk if you can. Not only does cold milk foam better, the foam lasts longer and tastes fresher.

Put the milk in a jug (filled no more than half way to allow it to expand) and immerse the steam wand right to the bottom of the jug to begin heating the milk. Then gradually raise it so that the nozzle is just under the surface of the milk. If it is too high you will spray the room with milk; if it is too low you will not get many bubbles. You should hear a hissing noise, rather than a rumble (which indicates that the nozzle is too deep). Do not use full power but do not be too timid, either. You do not want the milk to boil, but you do want to warm it through. The ideal result is a mass of small bubbles, which are more stable than bigger ones: any large bubbles should be knocked off or allowed to burst.

Finally, hold back the foam and add the hot milk from the bottom of the jug to the espresso, to come to about two-thirds of the way up the cup. Then spoon or scoop the foam you have just made for the top third of the drink. If you like a topping, such as chocolate or cinnamon, sprinkled on top, add it. Voilà—the perfect homemade cappuccino!

Place the steam jet just under the surface of the milk.

Gently spoon the froth on to the coffee.

Finish off with a sprinkle of chocolate powder.

Women enjoy an espresso at a coffee bar in the 1960s.

THE NEW FRONTIER: FULLY AUTOMATIC AND SINGLE-SERVE MACHINES

Nowadays, if you want to make an espresso drink, there is an alternative to fiddling with portable filters and tampers. You may have noticed in your local restaurant or specialty coffee store that when you order a coffee, the staff person often simply positions the cup under a spout in a modern-looking machine, pushes one button, and awaits the delivery of a (supposedly) perfect espresso. The fully automatic espresso machine grinds, tamps, and brews espresso—or longer coffee beverages—automatically, without the need for a traditional barista's expertise (and with far less mess).

These machines, which originated in Europe and are generally made in Switzerland, are beginning to replace the familiar semi-automatic, or "professional," machines that are mostly made in Italy. Although there is great debate over whether fully automatics can deliver better espresso than a good barista getting the best out of a traditional machine, it is no secret that their advantages have resulted in fully automatics catching on in restaurants and cafés all over Europe and increasingly in North America too. It was only a matter of time before smaller and more affordable versions came into common use in households, as they began to do in the late 1990s in Europe.

Besides saving on the mess and requiring much less expertise from the consumer who only wants to enjoy espresso drinks, the household machines—like their counterparts in coffee houses and restaurants—are much more flexible too. They allow the use of any type of coffee, because the consumer adds his or her own roasted beans to the hopper as required. Grinding is taken care of as well, eliminating the need for a separate unit, and the more modern machines also have a foaming wand (and perhaps even a refrigerated tank for storing milk), so that even a cappuccino or a latte are immediately available.

One step beyond the fully automatic machine is the single-serve machine, which combines the advantages of the fully automatic with the convenience of providing one cup when required. These machines eliminate the need for a grinder, by supplying the coffee pre-ground in individual pre-dosed pods (like a round tea bag) or hermetically sealed capsules, which merely have to be inserted into the unit. Water is then added (and can be controlled as required for an espresso or a longer coffee beverage).

Pod systems have been around for many years, and some of the better ones, such as Bunn's domestic range, are recommended today. However, the current single-serve phenomenon took hold on the household market with the capsule systems, first with Nestlé's successful Nespresso range of machines, introduced in the mid-1990s. More recently, the other main roasting groups—including Sara Lee, Procter & Gamble, and Kraft—have launched their own machines, and they supply coffee specifically for them. (One warning to those considering such a capsule machine: at the moment, despite mostly good reviews for the equipment, they operate in mutually exclusive closed systems—meaning that one coffee supplier's capsule or pod often will not fit in another's machine. You need to make sure you like the available range of coffees before buying a machine that will not be able to take anything else.)

THE CUPS

You may have a wonderful, state-of-the-art espresso machine, and you may be using perfectly ground, freshly roasted beans—but when it comes out of the machine, the coffee still may not be right. The *crema* may not have that smooth, creamy look. The problem could be that the cup was cold. Try storing the cups the right way up on top of the machine, so that they are warm from the bottom before you add the coffee: this also prevents burning your mouth on the top of an over-heated cup!

Fully automatic machine from the Nestlé Nespresso range, complete with capsules.

ESPRESSO MENU

Some of the other terms you will see on the menu board at your local café or espresso bar:

ESPRESSO RISTRETTO is made by "cutting off" the machine—that is, by switching it off sooner than in regular espresso so that the coffee is shorter (less liquid) and consequently denser, stronger, and more aromatic.

DOPPIO ("double") simply means two espresso shots in one cup.

AMERICANO is a normally brewed espresso that has been thinned by hot water, normally to the volume of a standard brewed cup of coffee.

CAFFÈ LATTE (or simply latte, one of the most popular espresso-based drinks) is made by adding milk, steamed to 150–170°F (65–76°C), to a freshly drawn shot of espresso. Sometimes served in a tall glass, it is finished with a ¼ inch (5 millimeters) layer of foamed milk and, if liked, a generous sprinkle of chocolate or cinnamon. This is basically a much milkier version of cappuccino.

ESPRESSO MACCHIATO is a basic espresso that is "marked" with just a little milk.

LATTE MACCHIATO is simply a glass of hot milk with a little espresso dribbled into it.

ESPRESSO ROMANO is espresso with a twist of lemon peel.

Latte art from a professional barista.

ESPRESSO CON PANNA is espresso with a spoonful of cold whipped cream.

CAFFÈ MOCHA (or simply mocha) is one-third espresso, one-third hot chocolate, and one-third steamed milk, added to the cup in that order. Nowadays, mochas are often made with a generous helping of a proprietary chocolate syrup—enough to coat the bottom of the cup—followed by a shot of espresso and the steamed milk. If you're feeling indulgent, the drink can be crowned with a scoop of whipped cream and lightly sprinkled with ground sweet cocoa. This drink is basically a chocolate cappuccino, and many other flavors of cappuccino exist as well: hazelnut, vanilla, or Irish Cream can all be created just by adding the appropriate syrup.

COLD COFFEE METHOD

This method is useful if you are making coffee that is going to be used in cold drinks, and it is always useful to have some in stock, especially during the summer. Mix a few tablespoons of ground coffee with about 2 pints (1 liter) of cold water and leave for 12 hours. Strain the liquid to remove the grounds and keep it in the refrigerator until you are ready to use it. It has a very strong flavor and will need to be watered down to individual taste. The extract will keep for several days in the refrigerator, and many people find beverages made from it easier to digest than regular coffee, because the gentle process extracts few oils and hardly any acidity from the coffee.

READY-TO-DRINK

Of course, there are alternatives if you are not prepared to make coffee yourself, but would like to enjoy it at home. Ready-made cold coffee drinks are now commonly available, often in sweetened form with milk added. In North America, this type of product was pioneered by Starbucks' bottled Frappuccino beverage, which is now available in supermarkets and convenience stores. A number of other products also exist, including Kraft's Cappio and various retailers' own brands, but almost all of these are cold, sweetened, and milky—and therefore seen as a way to get soft drink-loving teenagers and young adults interested in coffee.

The market for ready-to-drink coffee in cans is enormous in Japan and some other places in Asia, where vending machines dispense a huge range of coffee beverages (both hot and cold, and some in self-heating cans), alongside the more familiar soft drinks. This canned coffee market has yet to develop in North America, although there have been attempts to introduce it.

Kenco Cappio canned coffee (left) and Starbucks' Mocha Frappuccino (right).

BUYING COFFEE

Coffee beans on display at the Reading Terminal Market, Philadelphia.

Coffee began as a straight or single origin, and it was probably an "estate" coffee, if only because people consumed the coffee that was grown closest to them. As trade developed, however, blending took over, and today, although the best coffees from a single estate or an origin coffee from a specific country can be drunk "straight" (or unblended), coffee is essentially a blended drink—just as champagne, cognac, and some wines are. Indeed, some people would argue that the best coffee is achieved by blending the best characteristics from a range of different coffees—bright acidity from one, a floral aroma from another, full-bodied richness from a third—to make the best final product.

There have been times when blending has been something of an art form—Mocha Mysore is a popular blend of two quite different types of coffee, in which the soft richness of Mysore combines with the gamey flavor of Mocha—but on the whole it is done for commercial reasons.

Cheaper robusta is blended with arabica chiefly to reduce the price of the blend, and there can be no doubt that almost all blends are created to produce greater profit than if the individual coffees were sold separately.

The watchword in blending must be consistency. All commercial roasters are looking for continuity and consistency of flavor, and some regional roasters are known for their blends. It is good to experiment and try different coffee blends from various roasters in order to find your ideal flavor. The best introduction for a new coffee drinker might be a breakfast blend, which will be available from any good roaster. This is often made from a blend of African coffees for drinking with milk, or it might be a blend of two medium roasts of Kenyan and Colombian coffees to give a sharp, aromatic flavor to start the day. An after-dinner blend could come from the same source, but be darker roasted for extra strength. A strong but well-balanced after-dinner coffee might be a blend of mature coffee from Indonesia, made more racy and elegant by a touch of Kenyan and Costa Rican coffees.

The strongly flavored, very dark-roasted coffee blends have an apparent initial bitterness, but you soon get used to it. The most extreme instance of power in a cup would be a dark-roasted continental blend, which, when made as espresso, produces that coffee with the characteristic bitter bite that is popular with southern Italians—although, it has to be admitted, with few others. Espresso blends from north Italy are roasted to a lesser degree, and they have a delicate defining balance and acidity that is more akin to fine wine.

There is nothing to stop you creating your own blends. Various styles of blending are found in different parts of the world, some leaning toward heavy Sumatran coffees, while others may be dominated by an acidic Kenya or the winy quality of beans from Ethiopia. Central American coffees—because of their more neutral flavors—very often form the basis of most good blends. When you are faced with a choice of 15 or 20 coffees, how do you make an informed choice? As with wine, it is, of course, a personal matter, but it does pay to take advice from specialty coffee merchants, such as the members of the Specialty Coffee Association of America (SCAA) or the Speciality Coffee Association of Europe (SCAE).

Coffee roaster and Speciality Coffee Association of Europe president Colin Smith

Coffee beans on sale from Monmouth Coffee Company, Borough Market, London, England.

advises: "A blend of Central American coffees will always produce an ideal, all-day coffee as long as they are not roasted too dark. Such a blend may include Santos (Brazilian) for its mildness, Colombian for body, and Costa Rican for its fruity acidity. The fruitiness of Papua New Guinea with Sumatran and Mocha will produce a rich brew at a darker roast. The addition of robusta will add an earthy flavor and give the blend more body."

HANDLING AND STORING BEANS

In an ideal world you would probably buy small amounts of green beans (perhaps from a specialty roaster), roast them yourself, and grind them immediately before you want to make coffee. However, most of us have to buy roasted beans, often in larger quantities than we can use in just a few days.

When you have to store coffee beans, remember that the first main enemy is water. The volatile oils are water soluble—which gives us the flavor in the cup—but damp conditions will taint the oils. Do not store coffee in the refrigerator, because, once opened, moisture will condense on the surface of the container.

GUIDE TO THE WORLD'S MAIN ORIGIN COFFEES

SOUTH AMERICA

BRAZIL: the dominant force in the market, Brazil produces mainly mild, soft, and smooth coffees that can be used for blending—although recently, a huge range of specialty coffees have become available which are perfectly suited to drinking on their own.

COLOMBIA: full bodied and mellow, with a gentle acidity and slightly nutty flavor, this high-quality coffee comes from beans grown at high altitude.

CENTRAL AMERICA

COSTA RICA: mild, fragrant coffee with delicate acidity, grown mostly at high altitude.

GUATEMALA: the country's mountains and volcanic soil produce versatile coffee, which, when it is light roasted, is mild and full; when it is dark roasted, it becomes smoky and powerful.

CARIBBEAN

JAMAICA: Blue Mountain, the most famed of the island's coffees, is produced in tiny quantities at 5,000 feet (1,525 meters) above sea level. Very expensive, but at their best, very subtle coffees of great finesse.

EAST AFRICA

KENYA: the king of East African coffees, noted for its aroma and pleasant sharpness; this is good drunk black or with milk, when it retains its lively character.

TANZANIA: closer in flavor to the rich, delicate coffees of Central America; less acid than Kenyan coffee.

ETHIOPIA: the homeland of arabica, with many choices—Mocha has a strong, gamey flavor, while Yirgacheffe has a pronounced, wild taste with a unique tang.

ASIA

INDIA: an origin that offers a range of flavors—like the soft, rich Mysore, with low acidity and a light, winy taste, or Monsooned Malabar, which has a flavor which is used widely to make espresso.

INDONESIA: from its many islands, the origin presents a range of tastes from the heavy, mellow flavor of Java, to Sumatra, with its rich body and delicate acidity.

PAPUA NEW GUINEA: a coffee with a very fruity flavor and an unusual acidity.

If you have to store coffee for any length of time, it is better to put it in the freezer, making sure that it is in an airtight bag. Roasted beans that are to be kept for longer than a week should always be kept in the freezer. Do not try to thaw the beans when you need them—they can go straight from the freezer into the grinder.

The other great enemy of coffee is oxygen, which oxidizes the volatile flavors. This is why it is important to grind the beans immediately before you brew. Once coffee has been ground, much more of its surface is exposed to air, which means that oils begin to evaporate and the flavor vanishes into thin air.

Do not store coffee near to other strong-smelling or strongly flavored products. Like tea, coffee quickly picks up other scents and flavors. Store your coffee in an airtight, clean container that is reserved only for coffee.

If you buy coffee through mail order, only purchase small amounts at a time. Although you might save money through bulk buying, you will lose value as you lose flavor.

PACKAGING

The fresher the beans, the richer and more flavorful the cup. Coffee suppliers go to great lengths, therefore, to protect the freshly roasted beans from air, heat, light, and moisture, all of which impair the flavor.

In both Europe and the United States, the packaging of coffee has become something of a problem in itself. Not only are strict national regulations about the use of recyclable materials in force in many countries, but some countries within the European Union impose even tighter limits on the kinds of material that may be used. For example, aluminum, which was once widely used, has now fallen from favor in some markets. Combine this with increased consumer awareness of the costs—both in financial and environmental terms—of unnecessary packaging, and it is easy to see why many coffee companies are investing so much time and effort into rethinking their packaging policies.

Starbuck's Latin American breakfast blend beans, sold in a valve pack.

Single laminate packaging, with materials comprising many ultra-thin layers, is the mainstay of coffee nowadays, and in the United States, the traditional can has left the scene altogether—to be replaced by increasingly high-tech barrier films designed to protect the coffee. These laminated packages reduce both transport and environmental costs and some even allow consumers to reseal the bag with an enclosed zip-lock.

Most coffee packaging now uses specially designed one-way valve bags, into which the beans are packed soon after roasting. The valve on each bag allows the carbon dioxide, which is released by the freshly roasted beans, to escape, but prevents oxygen, which robs the beans of flavor, from entering.

Whatever the packaging, however, remember that, once opened, coffee must be stored in an airtight container in a cool, dry place.

FLAVORED COFFEES

At present, consumers have a choice of more than 100 different flavored coffees, which are produced by spraying beans (often the cheaper varieties) with carrier oils and covering them with flavoring after roasting. This trend began in the United States in the 1970s.

Favorite flavors are hazelnut, vanilla, chocolate, Irish Cream, amaretto, and various fruit essences. Coffee flavored with cardamom—which has long been added in the Middle East—is now available in many Western markets, and in Mexico, cinnamon is a popular and traditional addition that is also gaining interest elsewhere.

Smaller shops and serious coffee drinkers will need a separate grinder for flavored beans, because any residue will affect the taste of the next batch of unflavored beans that is ground. You might find it worthwhile to acquire an extra smaller, cheaper grinder if you develop a taste for flavored coffee, or just to buy pre-ground flavored coffee when you need it.

The three top flavors of essence coffee, which is widely available in France and the United States, are almond, vanilla, and hazelnut. These sell mostly in the hot summer months, when flavored iced coffee can be a refreshing beverage, and when regular coffee is drunk less often.

MILK

Besides sugar, the most commonly used flavoring in coffee is milk. Traditionally, in countries such as Yemen, Ethiopia, and Turkey, milk is never added to coffee, and it is not, of course, added to true espresso. It is thought that milk was first added to coffee in Grenoble, France, by Sieur Monin, in 1685.

The fats in full-cream milk will mask the subtle flavors of good coffee, so use half-fat or low-fat milk whenever possible. Carefully heating it is also a good idea, because hot (but not boiled) milk can add a delicious silkiness to coffee.

CAFFEINATED OR DECAF?

Those who claim that coffee does not taste the same without caffeine are only partly right. Caffeine is virtually tasteless; so the coffee will only taste different if any of the other elements that contribute to its flavor are taken out at the same time as the caffeine is removed.

Green beans that are to be decaffeinated are normally shipped to decaffeination plants from where, after treatment, they are shipped on to the roaster. It is quite possible for a bean grown in Mexico to be shipped to Switzerland, where it is decaffeinated, before being shipped back across the Atlantic to a roaster in San Diego.

Coffee is commonly decaffeinated using the solvent method, in which the beans are steamed to open them up, soaked in a solvent to dissolve the caffeine, and then steamed again to remove the traces of solvent.

The Swiss Water process, which was patented by Coffex SA in 1979, uses only water and carbon filters. This process involves soaking the beans in water, which removes the caffeine and the flavors. The caffeine is then separated from the water by an activated carbon filter, and the water, still containing the flavor, is evaporated and reduced to flavor concentrate, which is sprayed on to the dried beans.

If you want to cut down on your intake of caffeine but do not want to drink less coffee, one solution is to drink half and half—decaffeinated and regular—or try some of the available "half-caf" products, which are the same thing.

COFFEE DRINKING AROUND THE WORLD

Tourists enjoy a coffee next to the Rialto Bridge, Venice, Italy.

In the last few years, what is known as specialty coffee has swept the world. Consumers are gradually becoming more aware of origin coffees from around the globe, thanks in part to the spread of corner coffee bars, café chain stores, and espresso outlets. Tastes in coffee throughout the world have become increasingly sophisticated, as consumers are exposed to more interesting and exotic brews. Coffee, like wine before it, has become a "hip" beverage, and like wine, the same background of history and modern marketing help make it an attractive product to modern consumers. Coffee markets all over the world have their own distinctive characteristics, arising from the culture and history of the countries involved. However, there are a few examples that stand out as being the most interesting places to enjoy coffee and the local culture that goes along with it.

EUROPE

In Europe, as a general rule, northern markets prefer milder coffees and a lighter roast, served in brewed form. The further south you get, however, the darker and shorter the coffee becomes; culminating with the strong and black roasts of southern Italy and Spain.

SCANDINAVIA

Scandinavia has a tradition of importing high-quality coffee, and the result is that more coffee is consumed here than anywhere else. Finland, in particular, is known for its high levels of coffee consumption. It is traditional to offer coffee on any occasion, and that coffee is always freshly brewed.

BELGIUM

In Belgium, which has a strong chocolate tradition, a coffee ordered in a bar or café is not complete unless it is served with a small square of chocolate. The country has a large number of smaller coffee roasters, which serve local area bars and restaurants in the same way as those in Italy do.

ITALY

In Italy, the home of espresso, that word is never used, because a caffè always means an espresso. The short black beverage is ubiquitous, and most bars offer both alcoholic beverages and coffees side by side. The Italian term *barista*, meaning barman, is now used worldwide to denote an expert in the preparation of coffee, but in Italy and elsewhere in Europe, it means someone who is proficient in making all kinds of beverages. While it is still unusual in North American coffee bars, blending coffee and alcohol is common in many European markets, and the Coffee and Good Spirits competition, organized by the Speciality Coffee Association of Europe, recognizes the experts in this field.

FRANCE

France's tradition of the sidewalk café goes hand in hand with its coffee background, although even here the more modern specialty coffee bars are now beginning to compete for attention with the smoky and basic bars that have been the mainstay of coffee consumption previously.

Quintessential coffee shop in Cambridge, England.

GERMANY

The German-speaking countries—Germany, Austria, and northern Switzerland—are all big coffee consumers, with a tradition of mild coffees enjoyed at home and in smart cafés and restaurants.

UNITED KINGDOM

The United Kingdom, with its tea-drinking tradition, has a coffee market that is still dominated by instant coffee, although that is gradually changing as specialty coffee sweeps the country. The café culture of continental Europe is taking hold, and consumers are being offered a much broader range of coffees in supermarkets and other retail outlets as well.

EASTERN EUROPE

The newer coffee markets of Eastern Europe are now developing rapidly, as younger consumers are learning about and beginning to enjoy good coffee in markets where it was absent during the Soviet period. Russia, the Baltic countries, Poland, the Czech Republic, and Hungary are among those markets that are harking back to traditional coffee drinking, and combining that interest with the new Western specialty coffee brands.

Sidewalk café in the main square, Arras, France.

Cafés Manera poster from the 1930s (left). Café Malt poster from 1892 (right).

ASIA AND AUSTRALIA

In the Australasian markets, coffee is booming. In many countries in the region, traditional tea-drinking cultures are being invaded by the new coffee businesses—both roasters and retail chains—that have attracted strong interest among younger consumers.

JAPAN

Japan, which has a long tradition of coffee houses called *kissaten*, has developed into one of the fastest growing coffee markets in the world, as consumers with plenty of disposable income look for increasingly rare and exotic types of coffee. Much of the most sought-after coffee on earth ends up in the Japanese market, which takes more than 90 percent of Jamaica Blue Mountain, for example. The Japanese also invented canned coffee, which is dispensed by vending machines in hot and cold versions, making up a large sector of the market.

The rest of the Asian markets, including those of South Korea, Vietnam, and Thailand are seeing modern coffee houses springing up in the large cities, operated both by local roaster / retailers and by the representatives of familiar international chains.

AUSTRALIA

Australia—with its background of different immigrant ethnic groups influencing the market—has seen large growth in the coffee bar culture, and increasing sophistication in the retail coffee business that was originally dominated by instant coffee. With growing expertise in espresso on the coffee shop front, the country is also the source of a range of sought-after specialty green coffees.

CHINA

Of all the world markets, China has the most potential to develop into a big coffee consumer. At the moment, the growing middle classes in the largest cities are taking specialty coffee to their hearts in coffee bars and espresso houses. It remains to be seen whether the majority of the population will move toward coffee in a big way.

Vending machines dispense hot and cold coffee outside a local store in Japan.

The Starbucks sign stands out on a crowded street in Shanghai, China.

SOUTH AMERICA

A girl in ceremonial dress dances in the coffee-growing region of Armenia, Colombia.

Brazil is now the second largest consumer of coffee in the world by volume, and it will probably soon threaten the United States for the top position. After a quality revolution took place in the 1980s and 1990s, coffee consumption grew in leaps and bounds, and the country uses an increasing proportion of its own huge production for the local market.

AFRICA

Black coffee is poured in preparation for a traditional Ethiopian coffee ceremony.

In a continent where coffee is mostly grown as a cash crop for export, Ethiopia stands out as a result of consuming a large proportion of its own high-quality production. In the homeland of arabica, the coffee tradition carries on, with the crop often roasted, ground, and brewed by hand, to be enjoyed by a broad cross-section of the population.

UNITED STATES

Coffee has probably been an American mainstay since the Boston Tea Party, before the War of Independence, and, although in general the United States is not a nation of quality coffee drinkers, there is a large and growing market for specialty coffees.

In the 1960s the situation was very different, for the market, concentrated in the hands of a few suppliers, was saturated with poor quality, cheap coffee. It was this situation that caused the original rise of the specialty coffee sector, which started in the early 1980s when a diverse group of small roasters and green coffee suppliers assembled to form the Specialty Coffee Association of America (SCAA). Advocating the use of only good quality green coffee and care in roasting, the group let their products speak for themselves. Eventually, their philosophy (and the vast improvement they were offering over

run-of-the-mill coffee) caught on with consumers, so that the 1980s and 1990s saw the rise of the specialty coffee bar chains, dominated by Starbucks, but including regional roasters and retailers in all of the major markets.

Seattle was the original home of Starbucks, and the northwestern United States remains the heartland of the specialty coffee movement, and here, espresso-based drinks dominate. The espresso beans consumed in the United States may require a higher roast because of the national taste for 100 percent arabica beans in espresso. In Italy and France, on the other hand, the proportion of arabica to robusta can be as high as half and half. When arabica beans are dark roasted, they tend to release more acidity into the brew, so they usually have to be extra-high roasted to balance this acidity. Beans with a stronger flavor have become increasingly

Drive-thru coffee with a difference, California.

popular in the United States—led by the dark roasts favored by Starbucks and others in the northwest—although some coffee connoisseurs regret this, because it becomes harder to distinguish the subtleties of different origins' flavor characteristics in dark-roast beans.

In the specialty outlets, espresso is the usual coffee style on offer, even on the streets, following the enormous growth in the number of carts or mobile espresso bars. The specialty business fits well into the country's take-away culture, but it also offers an alternative place to relax in pleasant surroundings. To begin with, an espresso bar—or even a cart—was seen as an attractive investment for novices, but most of these outlets disappeared as the need for hard work, good training, and significant investment soon became clear.

Consumer demand for specialty coffee in the United States, after two decades of growth, continues to develop, according to the SCAA (which currently has around 3,000 member companies and as such is the largest coffee organization in the world). In 2005, the specialty coffee sector was worth just over $11 billion, and there were an estimated 21,400 specialty coffee outlets (cafés, espresso bars, and retail stores) operating. There are still 10 percent more independent sector outlets than cafés run by the specialty chains. It is estimated that 15 percent of American adults drink specialty coffee daily (while 60 percent drink it occasionally). In general, specialty coffee has reversed the downward trend in American coffee consumption, and it still appears as one of the few sectors that remains strong.

Americans drink more than 300 million cups of coffee daily, and the country is, by volume, the largest consumer of coffee on earth (followed by Brazil, the second largest consumer, which looks like catching up in the next few years). Most of the coffee drunk in the United States today comes from Brazil, Vietnam, Colombia, Guatemala, and Mexico.

Bags are filled with coffee beans at Zabar's, New York City.

STARBUCKS

The coffee "revolution" began in the 1970s in Seattle—possibly because that city enjoys good, clean water—and Starbucks quickly became the city's second most famous export (Boeing being the first). The company, founded by Gordon Bowker (whose idea it was), Jerry Baldwin, and Zev Siegl, took its name from a character in Herman Melville's novel, *Moby-Dick*. Zev Siegl went to Berkeley, California, to train with one of the specialty coffee pioneers, Alfred Peet, who had experience in both coffee and tea from around the world and from whom, initially, Starbucks bought roasted coffees. The first Starbucks store opened in Pike Place Market in central Seattle in 1971.

Howard Schultz, who was eventually to acquire the company, joined in 1982, and a trip to Milan the following year established his aim to bring the Italian coffee bar experience to the United States. After the original owners acquired Peet's, they sold Starbucks to Schultz in 1987, when the chain had just 17 outlets. Starbucks expanded rapidly, and by 1990 had moved beyond Seattle, to open stores in Denver, Chicago, and Washington. The company went public in 1992, raising around $110 million, much of which was invested in opening new outlets; it had 165 at the end of that year. After opening a second roasting plant in 1993, Starbucks established a relationship with book

The original Starbucks in Seattle, as it was in 1971.

The original Starbucks in Seattle, as it looks today.

retailer Barnes and Noble, which saw its outlets in most of the bookseller's stores. Starbucks first moved on to the international market with a joint venture company in Japan in 1996, when it already had more than 1,000 outlets in North America. It acquired a British-based chain to launch itself into Europe, and then developed markets in China and most of the other important Asian countries. By the end of 2006, the ubiquitous Starbucks plans to have 11,215 outlets worldwide.

Trading on the concept of "the third place" apart from home and work, the company has strived to offer a comfortable alternative venue for coffee, and has expanded its offering greatly in recent years to take in coffee-making accessories, its own music label, and a number of other consumer product lines. However, the coffee, both in bean and beverage form, is still the company's primary offering, and it continues routinely to buy—often at well over market prices—some of the best green coffee in the world. It roasts in the United States as well as in Amsterdam, and buys its green coffee through its company in Lausanne, Switzerland. It has developed its own system of working directly with growers and estates at origin, rewarding those that offer consistent quality and sustainable production. Starbucks has also formed an alliance with the Fairtrade Labelling Organization to sell Fair Trade Certified coffee in the countries where it operates.

Starbucks also has a reputation for roasting its coffee the darkest of the U.S. roasters, although it appears in general that the demand for this roast level has increased significantly in America and elsewhere. Certainly the numbers of customers passing through Starbucks' doors worldwide suggest that the consumers themselves like what they find there.

GETTING THE BEST COFFEES FROM THE BEST SPECIALTY ROASTERS

It goes against the grain for most of the good specialty roasters to be represented in supermarkets, but nowadays, there are a number of other outlets, including mail order and Internet "e-tailers," that offer freshly roasted coffee (as well as equipment and other necessary supplies). Of course, virtually all roasters with retail shops will sell their coffee beans in their own outlets, and many restaurants that use special customized blends from local wholesale roasters often sell those blends on-site as well. Among other sources are the websites for organic grocery chain Whole Foods Market, and for the specialty foods retailer Dean & DeLuca.

Among the coffee suppliers with the highest reputations are Starbucks itself, with its large and thriving mail order business; F Gaviña & Sons from the Los Angeles area; Allegro from Boulder, Colorado, which has a strong organic business; Batdorf & Bronson from Washington state; Intelligentsia of Chicago; Portland, Oregon's Stumptown; specialty coffee pioneer George Howell's Terroir from Acton, Massachusetts; Zoka, Victrola, and Espresso Vivace, all of Seattle; Kansas City's The Roasterie; Gimme Coffee from Ithaca, New York; Supreme Bean in North Hollywood, California; Kean Coffee in Newport Beach, California, run by coffee-roasting veteran Martin Diedrich; Counter Culture Coffee in Durham, North Carolina; Green Mountain Coffee Roasters from Vermont; Caribou Coffee based in Minneapolis; and Peet's Coffee & Tea, one of the longest established and most appreciated roasters, from Burlingame, California. The web addresses of all these companies are listed in the Useful Links section at the end of the book.

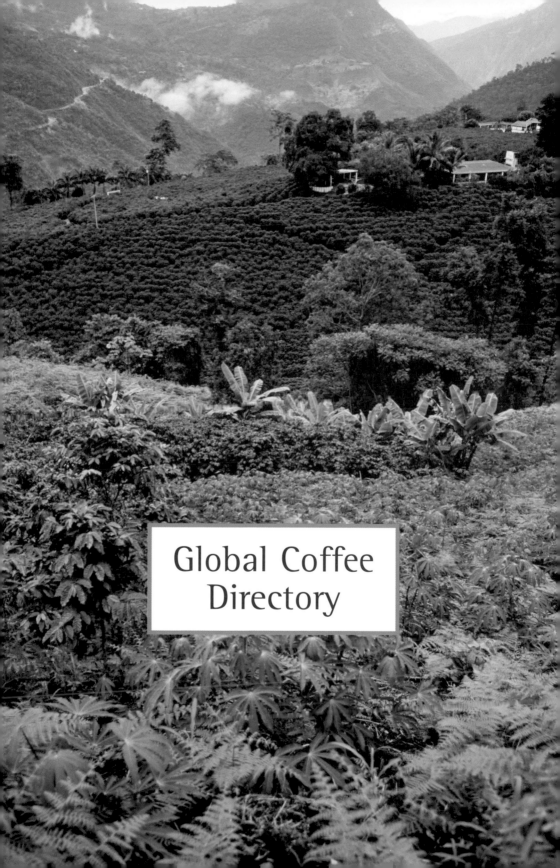

Global Coffee Directory

MAIN COFFEE PRODUCING COUNTRIES OF THE WORLD

1 Costa Rica
2 Cuba
3 Dominican Republic
4 El Salvador
5 Guatemala
6 Haiti

7 Honduras
8 Jamaica
9 Mexico
10 Nicaragua
11 Panama
12 Puerto Rico

13 Bolivia
14 Brazil
15 Colombia
16 Ecuador
17 Galapagos Islands
18 Peru

19 Venezuela
20 Angola
21 Burundi
22 Cameroon
23 Democratic Republic
    of Congo

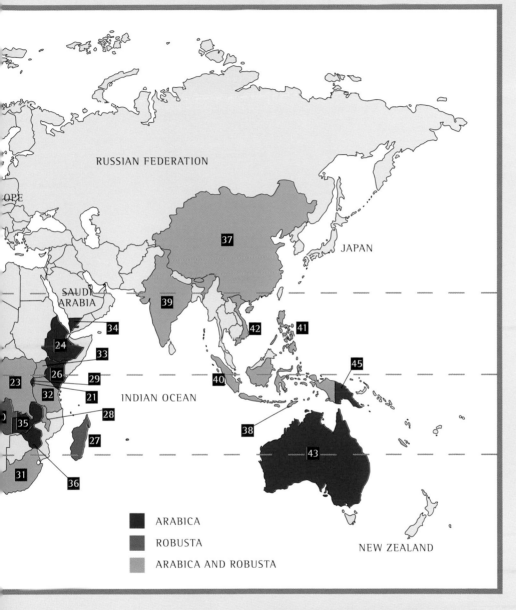

ARABICA

ROBUSTA

ARABICA AND ROBUSTA

24 Ethiopia	30 St Helena	36 Zimbabwe	42 Vietnam
25 Ivory Coast	31 South Africa	37 China	43 Australia
26 Kenya	32 Tanzania	38 East Timor	44 Hawaii (U.S.A.)
27 Madagascar	33 Uganda	39 India	45 Papua New Guinea
28 Malawi	34 Yemen	40 Indonesia	
29 Rwanda	35 Zambia	41 Philippines	

This country-by-country guide covers the major coffee-producing
countries in the world whose coffees are generally available
to the general public.

STAR RATINGS

Each entry is given an overall star quality rating: fair, good, or
excellent. The star rating refers to the origin as a whole and not to
particular regions or estates.

   ★ ★ ★   Excellent

   ★ ★   Good

   ★   Fair

FLAVOR PROFILE

These information boxes accompany each entry in the directory and
give a brief description of the flavor of that particular coffee, and a
suggested roast (incorporating suggested uses where applicable).
The profile also includes at-a-glance information about the most
important constituents that together make up the flavor. These are:
body, acidity, and balance (see Tasting Coffee in the first part of the
book for a full explanation of these terms).

FLAVOR: full bodied with a lush, smoky flavor

SUGGESTED ROAST: medium to high; excellent for blending

BODY	⧗ ⧗ ⧗ ⧗
ACIDITY	⧗ ⧗ ⧗ ⧗
BALANCE	⧗ ⧗ ⧗ ⧗

CENTRAL AMERICA
AND
THE CARIBBEAN

COSTA RICA
✭✭✭

*Good acidity and a tangy aroma combined
with full bodied richness.*

I n many people's opinion, Costa Rican Tarrazu is one of the world's greatest coffees. It has a light, clean flavor and a wonderful fragrance.

Costa Rica, with its rich, well-drained, volcanic soil, was the first Central American country to grow coffee and bananas on a commercial basis and both commodities are among its major exports. Coffee was introduced to Costa Rica from Cuba in 1729, and today the industry is one of the best organized in the world with a high yield of around 1,520 pounds per acre (1,700 kilograms per hectare). The population of Costa Rica is 3.5 million; about 12 percent of whom actually works in the coffee industry. There are 400 million coffee trees and, not surprisingly, the good, highly consistent coffee represents a significant share of the country's export earnings. Costa Rica benefits from the presence in Turrialba of the Central American Agricultural Research Institute (IAAC), which is an important international research center. The country is also the home of

☕ FLAVOR PROFILE ☕

FLAVOR: excellent, silky with full acidity and accessible class; beguiling aroma.

SUGGESTED ROAST: medium; can be high roasted.

BODY	🫘 🫘 🫘 🫘
ACIDITY	🫘 🫘 🫘 🫘 🫘
BALANCE	🫘 🫘 🫘 🫘

one of the foremost gatherings in the coffee industry, the so-called "coffee week" of Sintercafé, which brings together most of the region's important producers and its main customers every November.

Only arabica beans are grown; growing robusta coffee is illegal. The best Costa Rican coffee is labeled "SHB"—strictly hard bean—

which means that it has been grown at an altitude above 5,000 feet (1,500 meters). Altitude is often a problem for coffee growers. It is acknowledged that higher altitudes produce better beans; not only because they have the effect of increasing the acidity of the bean and thereby improving the flavor, but also because the cold nights that occur at higher altitudes mean that the trees mature more slowly, allowing the beans to develop a fuller flavor. The regular rainfall that is caused by precipitation at the higher altitudes is also essential for the proper development of the trees. However, these advantages have to be offset against the additional transportation involved, which can increase costs to such an extent that the beans become uneconomical to produce. The Costa Rican industry has adopted new mechanical ways to improve efficiency, including the use of electronic color sorting to identify and reject irregularly sized beans.

Just south of the capital, San José, is Tarrazu, one of the country's most highly regarded coffee-growing areas. La Minita Tarrazu, one of the world's best known specialty coffees, is produced in limited quantities—about 289,000 pounds each year—on an estate called La Minita owned, for the last three generations, by the McAlpin family. Their coffee is grown without the use of artificial fertilizers or pesticides and it is harvested and sorted separately and by hand.

Other good names to look out for are Juan Vinas (PR), H. Tournon, Windmill (SHB), Monte Bello, and Santa Rosa, and fine coffee is grown in Heredia and in the Central Valley. Another name to watch for is Sarchi, which is just one of five towns representing Costa Rica's "road of coffee." FJO Sarchi is grown on the slopes of Volcano Poás, which is about 33 miles (53 kilometers) from San José. Central Valley, Tres Rios, Alajuela, and Naranjo are the other main growing regions in the country.

The country's coffee industry is controlled by the Instituto del Cafe de Costa Rica (ICAFE). Meanwhile, the Specialty Coffee Association of Costa Rica represents the high-quality producers, and organizes the Cosecha de Oro, an internationally judged contest to find the country's best coffees every harvest. The winning coffees are offered by Internet auction and bought by the top specialty traders and roasters around the world.

Costa Rican workers wait in line to measure baskets of freshly harvested coffee.

CUBA
★ ★

*It would be surprising if Cuba did not produce
good coffee to accompany its fine cigars.*

The best Cuban coffee is Turquino or Extra Turquino. Turquino is a grade rather than a district, such as Jamaica's Blue Mountain, and the beans are grown in the center and east of the island. The coffee is clean tasting and medium bodied, and it has a lower acidity than many of the coffees grown in Central America because it is grown at a lower altitude.

Despite a promising start in the mid-eighteenth century, the future of Cuban coffee cannot be foretold. Certainty of supply and consistent quality cannot be assured in the present political climate. However, once these problems have been resolved, there is no doubt that Cuba could become an important source for both the United States and Japan.

Waiting for take-out coffee, Cuba.

🫘 FLAVOR PROFILE 🫘

FLAVOR: full bodied with a lush, smoky flavor.

SUGGESTED ROAST: medium to high; excellent for blending.

BODY

ACIDITY

BALANCE

DOMINICAN REPUBLIC
✱ ✱

*Coffee that is pleasantly sweet
and has good body.*

The Dominican Republic shares the island of Hispaniola with Haiti, and, like its neighbor, the country has a history of revolution and poverty. Democratic elections have now been held and some stability has been introduced.

Coffee was first grown in the Dominican Republic in the early eighteenth century. The best producing region is the southwest, in the region of Barahona, but fine coffee is also grown in Juncalito and Ocoa. The coffees, which are sometimes called Santo Domingo, are mild and full bodied, with good acidity and a pleasing aroma. Unlike the coffee produced in Haiti, most of the coffee produced in the Dominican Republic is washed; an indication of its higher overall quality.

Central Highlands, Dominican Republic.

🫘 FLAVOR PROFILE 🫘

FLAVOR: balanced with fair acidity.

SUGGESTED ROAST: medium to high roast; good, all-around coffee with many uses.

BODY	🫘🫘
ACIDITY	🫘🫘🫘
BALANCE	🫘🫘🫘🫘

EL SALVADOR

*Exclusively arabica coffee that
is mild in flavor.*

Not only is El Salvador one of the smallest countries in Central America, it is also one of the most densely populated, with about 10 percent of the people—some 650,000—involved in coffee growing or exporting. It produces balanced, if not distinctive coffee, which today accounts for only about 15 percent of the country's exports. In the first half of the twentieth century, the country had been almost completely dependent on the coffee industry. The best coffee is exported between January and March, with Germany taking a large share of the finest quality, the SHG.

The guerrilla war of the 1980s and more recent unrest, as well as disrupting the nation's economy generally, did much, indirectly, to encourage the spread of coffee rust and coffee borer. As a result, production fell from around 3.5 million bags in the early 1970s to about 2.5 million between 1990 and 1991. The eastern parts of the country were the worst affected, causing many farmers and workers to flee from the plantations. El Salvador was one of the producing countries hit badly by the coffee price crisis of the late 1990s and early years of this decade, and it has been estimated that many tens of thousands of coffee growers were thrown out of work because of the continuing

🫘 FLAVOR PROFILE 🫘

FLAVOR: well-balanced flavor; good characteristics.

SUGGESTED ROAST: medium to high; many uses.

BODY

ACIDITY

BALANCE

View over plantations in El Salvador, with ripe coffee cherries on a branch in the foreground.

low prices; consequently, huge numbers of farms went out of production.

El Salvador's coffee is typical of Central America—it is light bodied, aromatic, clean, and has light acidity. As in Guatemala and Costa Rica, coffee is graded according to altitude; the higher the altitude, the better. The best known brand name is Pipil, an Aztec-Mayan name for coffee, which is recognized by the Organic Certified Institute of America. An unusual bean is the Pacamara, a hybrid of the Pacas and Maragogype, and the best production is in the west of the country, around Santa Ana, which is close to the border with Guatemala. Pacamara gives an exceptionally fine cup of coffee, which is full bodied but not too heavy and fragrant. More recently, specialty traders and roasters have been finding new varieties from the country, including from the Las Delicias and Santa Barbara estates, as well as certified organic coffees like San Antonio.

Drying coffee parchment.

GUATEMALA
★ ★ ★

The strictly hard bean is full bodied and deliciously balanced—a spicy, complex cup.

Guatemala is one of the world's top coffee origins, and, as the world's eighth largest producer, is a major supplier to the United States, with a range of coffees from mainstream to exceptional specialty types.

Coffee trees were introduced to the country in 1750 by Jesuit priests, and the industry was developed by German settlers in the late nineteenth century. Today, most production is carried out in the south of the country, where the slopes of the volcanic mountains in the Sierra Madre provide ideal conditions for fine-quality arabica beans. The high altitude produces wonderfully lively coffee, and connoisseurs often prefer the spicy, complex flavor to other kinds of bean. The SHB coffee is among the best you can find: full bodied with deliciously balanced acidity. Elephant beans have also earned Guatemala a lot of attention, while several American roasters source specialties from the sought-after areas of Antigua and Huehuetenango.

Coffee initially made the country prosperous, and still employs about a third of the working population. Unfortunately, the unstable political situation within the country has not always benefited the coffee growers. Yields, which are often a good indication of a country's overall economy, are comparatively low at 625 pounds per acre (700 kilograms per hectare). In El Salvador, on the other hand, the yield is 800

☕ FLAVOR PROFILE ☕

FLAVOR: full, attractive, spicy, and complete.

SUGGESTED ROAST: medium; can be high roasted.

BODY	●●●●
ACIDITY	●●●●
BALANCE	●●●●

pounds per acre (900 kilograms per hectare), and in Costa Rica it is an astonishing 1,520 pounds per acre (1,700 kilograms per hectare). The export trade is in the hands of private companies, but the Asociación Nacional del Café (Anacafé) controls all other aspects of the industry.

Most of the smaller producers (naturales) are of Mayan descent and have been the subject of a number of aid programs—many funded by the United States and other foreign governments, and by large roasting concerns—designed to encourage specialty coffee production. The aim has been to help overcome the cycle of high-yield, low-quality plants that besets coffee production throughout the world. Many of these schemes also encourage local producers to process their own beans, with assistance in setting up and running small mills. Still, most of the red cherries are sold to middlemen, often just at the roadside, but it is felt that more added value for small producer cooperatives, and even increased quality, will result if processing is carried out in local mills.

The Maya Nuevo cooperative, which supplies the exporter Unitrade, is an example of how aid—in this case partly from the European Union—is helping local farmers to benefit more directly from their quality coffee. Located on Lake Atitlan and surrounded by volcanoes, the cooperative has 72 members, and produces fancy SHBs at an altitude of 5,300 feet (1,615 meters). The beneficio, as the mills in Guatemala are known, produces about four containers of coffee each crop.

Antigua, a small region located around the colonial capital city with the same name, is the best-known coffee region. Its coffees are so sought after that the local growers have banded together to form the genuine Antigua area, certifying the origin of their coffee in the same way a fine wine region would. The Finca Bella Vista is one of the region's best farms, and has the awards and the customers—including Starbucks—to prove it. Run by the Zelaya family,

Roadside sale, Guatemala.

the farm and its nearby neighbors produce Santa Ana la Huerta, Bella Carmona, and Pulcal; all genuine Antiguas that have had international success. Antiguas generally are not only of excellent quality but have a fuller, smokier, more complex flavor than other Guatemalan coffees. About every 30 years, the area around Antigua is subject to serious volcanic eruptions, which provide additional nitrogen to the already rich soil—although the dramatic surrounding mountains belch smoke more or less continuously. The area is further blessed by light, frequent rainfall, and strong sunshine.

Anacafé, taking advantage of the ideal coffee-growing conditions in the country, has grouped Guatemalan coffee into a number of regions related to microclimates. Besides Antigua, there are Fraijanes plateau near the capital, the humid rainforest region of Cobán, Huehuetenango in the highlands, Atitlan around the lake, as well as San Marcos, and Nuevo Oriente. Each region has its own special characteristics worth exploring.

HAITI
★

*Good coffee from a politically
troubled country.*

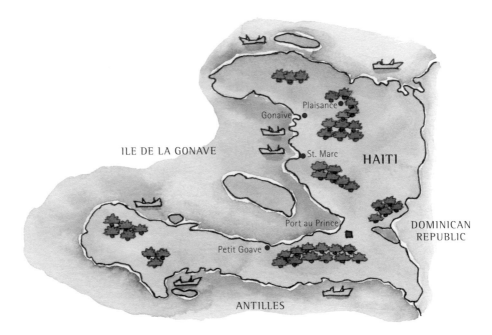

Despite its well-publicized problems Haiti manages to produce some good coffee, although the quality is variable.

Much of the coffee produced here is organic, although not all is certified that way. This is less by design than by default, because the farmers are often too poor to buy fungicides, pesticides, and fertilizers. The main growing area is in the north of the country but, more than almost any other producer, Haiti has developed a multiplicity of names, classifications, and types.

Not only does Haitian coffee have the distinction of being used in Japan to add to Jamaican Blue Mountain to make it go further, but it is also starting to get a name for itself on its own. This is thanks to Haitian Bleu, which was developed in the mid-1990s as a premium coffee—based on the same typica variety grown since coffee was imported into the country in the eighteenth century. A number of U.S. and international specialty roasters are now buying Haitian Bleu.

The coffee itself is heavy bodied and quite full flavored, with mid to low acidity and a somewhat soft flavor.

☕ FLAVOR PROFILE ☕

FLAVOR: balanced and dense.

SUGGESTED ROAST: medium; good high roast, especially for espresso.

BODY   🫘🫘🫘🫘

ACIDITY   🫘🫘

BALANCE   🫘🫘🫘🫘

HONDURAS
✦ ✦

Honduran coffee is generally a well-regarded blending coffee.

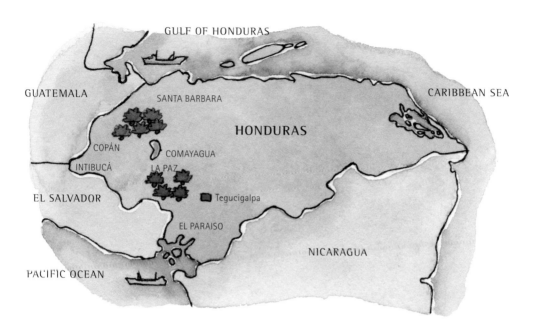

Coffee was originally brought to Honduras from El Salvador, and the country now produces good quality coffee, often with good acidity. A combination of the coffee crisis, politics, and some recent severe climate events has reduced production from a decade ago, but there are now more than 40,000 coffee farms, and it is thought that at least 0.5 million people depend on the crop.

Coffee rust has proved to be a hazard, especially in the east of the country. The copper sprays used to treat this disease have had the unexpected benefit of increasing yields.

As elsewhere, classification depends on altitude. In Honduras, coffee grown at 2,300 to 3,280 feet (700 to 1,000 meters) is known as Central Standard; that grown at 3,280 to 4,900 feet (1,000 to 1,500 meters) is known as High Grown; and that grown at 4,900 to 6,560 feet (1,500 to 2,000 meters) is Strictly High Grown. Among the SHGs, Yoija, La Central (a fair trade and organic coffee), and Marcala are known in the trade, although the origin is still mostly used for blending.

☕ FLAVOR PROFILE ☕

FLAVOR: good, soft; useful for blending and as a single.

SUGGESTED ROAST: medium to high; many uses.

BODY	🫘	🫘	🫘
ACIDITY	🫘	🫘	🫘
BALANCE	🫘	🫘	🫘

JAMAICA
★ ★ ★

*Is Jamaica Blue Mountain the best coffee in the world,
or the most over-rated?*

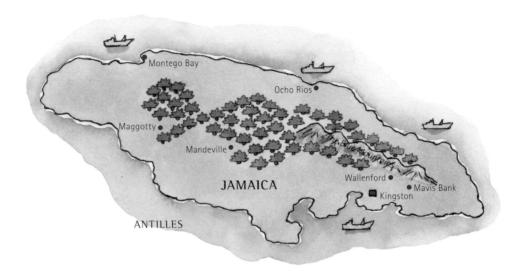

Jamaica produces coffee other than Blue Mountain, but almost everyone who has heard of Jamaica Blue Mountain knows that it is the most expensive coffee in the world. Not everyone knows why. When an article—whether it is a Rolls-Royce or a Stradivarius violin—acquires a reputation as being "the best in the world," the reputation tends to develop a life of its own and it becomes something of a self-perpetuating myth. In a complicated world, a simplification is often welcome.

At its best there can be no doubt that Blue Mountain is one of the very best coffees available. The price, however, does not reflect the "better" flavor as much as the premium that some people are prepared to pay to secure supplies of it. It is also worth remembering that this coffee is even more expensive to drink than it seems—to enjoy the flavor at its best you have to use more beans per cup than for other coffees. If you do not, the flavor can seem a little hollow. So the real cost of the flavor is the

difference between it and the next most expensive coffee, plus 10 or 15 percent for the extra beans needed.

That said, however, real Blue Mountain coffee, which comes from the appropriately best, local, blue-green beans, is a connoisseur's delight. The flavor is full, although very mild: it has balance, fruit, and acidity and provides all the satisfaction one could want. The aroma is intense and strong, but above all the flavor of good, fresh Blue Mountain is unusually persistent and, as wine drinkers might say, develops on the palate.

It is worth looking closely at the myth of Blue Mountain, for past image and present reality are not always the same. The first trees were brought to Jamaica from Martinique in 1725. They were imported by Sir Nicholas Lawes and planted in St. Andrew parish, which is still one of the three Blue Mountain parishes, the other two being Portland and St. Thomas. Within eight years more than 83,000 pounds (375,000 kilograms) of

JAMAICA
* * *

Jamaican coffee plantation in the ominous shadow of the Blue Mountains.

clean beans were being exported. Production peaked in 1932 when more than 33 million pounds (15 million kilograms) were grown.

By 1948, however, the quality of the coffee had deteriorated to such an extent that Canadian buyers refused to renew their contracts, and the Jamaican government established the Coffee Industry Board to revive the industry's fortunes. By 1969 matters had improved sufficiently for Japanese loans to be offered to improve production quality and to guarantee a market. Even in 1969 Japanese coffee drinkers were willing to pay a premium price for this coffee—and today it enjoys something approaching cult status.

By 1981, a further 3,500 acres (1,500 hectares) had been brought into cultivation, and this was followed by the financing of an additional 15,000 acres (6,000 hectares). Today the Blue Mountain region is, in fact, only a tiny growing area of around 15,000 acres (6,000 hectares), and it is impossible for all the coffee

Distinctive packaging for the famous
Jamaican Blue Mountain coffee.

labeled "Blue Mountain" to have originated there. The area outside the certified Blue Mountain region produces two other coffees—High Mountain Supreme and Prime Washed Jamaican.

True Blue Mountain coffee is one of the highest grown coffees in the world, and the climate, geology, and topology of Jamaica combine to provide the ideal location. The spine of mountains that runs across Jamaica ends in the east of the island in the Blue Mountains, which reach to more than 7,000 feet (2,100 meters). The climate is cool and misty, with frequent rainfall, and the rich soil is well drained. Terracing and mixed cropping are used, with coffee growing alongside bananas and avocado pears.

It is available from estates such as the Wallenford, Mavis Bank, and Moy Hall. However, even the largest growers in the area are small by international standards, and many are smallholders whose families have worked the land for two centuries. The industry faces problems from increasing labor costs and from the fact that the nature of the terrain makes mechanization difficult. The numerous small estates and farms also make rationalization of production difficult. Additionally, Jamaica is prone to hurricanes and has been hit (and severely affected) by many of the storms that seem to hit the region more regularly and with increasing ferocity. In 2005, Hurricanes Dennis and Emily caused serious damage to the Blue Mountain region's infrastructure and the result was a further reduction in availability for an already rare coffee.

Blue Mountain is, nevertheless, the one coffee that virtually all self-respecting coffee retailers stock, because it sells consistently throughout the year, despite the price.

The Japanese now buy up to 90 percent of the crop. With only 10 percent available for the rest of the world there is always going to be a shortfall, whatever the price. Blue Mountain is distinguished from other coffees by being transported in wooden barrels that contain 154 pounds (70 kilograms). The barrels—which were copied from the Bonifieur produced on Guadeloupe in the last century and were originally the barrels in which flour had been sent to Jamaica from Britain—always bear the brand names or appellations of the processing factory. The Coffee Industry Board certifies all pure Jamaican coffee and issues a seal of authenticity before it is exported.

🫘 FLAVOR PROFILE 🫘

FLAVOR: very full, with prominent fruit flavors.

SUGGESTED ROAST: medium.

BODY	🫘🫘🫘🫘
ACIDITY	🫘🫘🫘
BALANCE	🫘🫘🫘🫘

MEXICO
* *

*Smooth, fragrant coffee from the seventh
largest producer in the world.*

The seventh largest coffee producer in the world, Mexico has an annual production of about 4 million bags. Most of the coffee is produced by indigenous people on around 100,000 small farms, and the great estates that once dominated the industry are rare today. Here, politics is never far away from coffee. The growing area of Chiapas, in the south of the country, has been a hotbed of unrest for many years and the widely publicized uprising in the 1990s involved many whose main livelihood was coffee production.

The Instituto Mexicano del Café (Inmecafé), which both controlled the areas planted with coffee and marketed the beans, now has a more limited role. Meanwhile, the North America Free Trade Agreement (NAFTA) has been beneficial for Mexican exports, especially to the United States, where it is one of the main suppliers.

Mexico is one of the largest producers of organic coffee, and is also significantly involved in various ethical movements—Utz Kapeh,

Rainforest Alliance, and Fairtrade coffee are all available. Mexican Maragogype (elephant) beans are sought after, as are some of the SHG types.

The best region is Chiapas, where the brand names include Tapachula and Huixtla. Oaxaca (also in the south) produces fine beans, and is the home for organically grown Pluma. From Veracruz, farther north, Altura Orizaba and Altura Huatusco are notable.

🫘 FLAVOR PROFILE 🫘

FLAVOR: smooth and fragrant with good, mellow depth of flavor.

SUGGESTED ROAST: excellent as high roast.

BODY	🫘🫘🫘🫘
ACIDITY	🫘🫘🫘🫘
BALANCE	🫘🫘🫘🫘

NICARAGUA

*The very best Nicaraguan coffees are among the finest in the world
—mild, mid-bodied, and very fragrant.*

Political problems have, in so many countries, badly affected coffee production, and the Nicaraguan coffee industry is no exception. The 1979 revolution caused some of the large coffee plantation owners to flee to Miami; then followed a period of indecision while the government decided whether the land, including the coffee plantations, should be redistributed. This led to a disruption in supply, with production falling from more than 1 million bags in the early 1970s to fewer than 600,000 in 1990.

Although the industry has now been freed from government restraint and marketing is in the hands of private companies, problems remain, as the country gets to grips with the results of land reform, the coffee crisis, and the ever-present political problems.

The best Nicaraguan coffees are grown in the north and center of the country, and the best of all come from Matagalpa, Jinotega, and Nuevo Segovia. The Proodecoop group of cooperatives, which represents about 2,500 growers and their families, produces strictly high grown coffees under the Fairtrade scheme, and this is a single origin coffee which is available from specialty coffee outlets. The best Nicaraguan coffees, which are classified as Central Estrictamente Altura, are very satisfying, with good acidity and fine fragrance. The more average beans are widely used in blends.

❦ FLAVOR PROFILE ❦

FLAVOR: good blending beans; the top-quality beans are very fragrant.

SUGGESTED ROAST: excellent high-roast beans; good for espresso.

BODY	●●
ACIDITY	●●●
BALANCE	●●●

PANAMA
★ ★

*Specialty coffees come into
their own.*

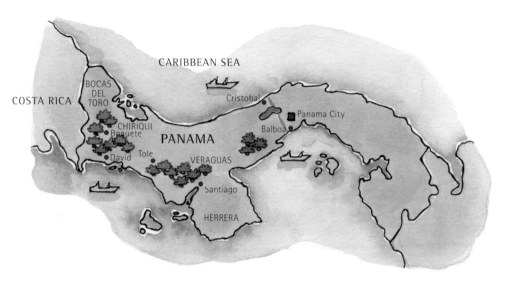

Coffee from Panama is famously smooth, light bodied, and very balanced, and the highest quality beans offer real character and good flavor.

Founded in 1997, the Specialty Coffee Association of Panama (SCAP) proved that the country's coffee has come into its own in the past few years. Its members are the best specialty coffee growers, with farm sizes ranging from 2.5 acres (less than a hectare) of coffee to 250 acres (more than 100 hectares). The SCAP organized the Best of Panama competition and Internet auction which, in May 2006, netted an unheard-of price of more than $50 a pound for the winning coffee from Hacienda La Esmeralda in western Panama.

The finest beans are grown in the north of the country, near to the border with Costa Rica and on the Pacific side. The Boquete district in Chiriqui province produces notable coffee, and the other districts to look out for are David, Remacimeinto, Bugaba, and Tole.

Beans are spread out to dry naturally, Panama.

🌰 FLAVOR PROFILE 🌰

FLAVOR: good quality with a full body.

SUGGESTED ROAST: medium.

BODY	🫘🫘🫘🫘
ACIDITY	🫘🫘🫘
BALANCE	🫘🫘🫘🫘

99

PUERTO RICO
★ ★ ★

*The Caribbean island with some of
the world's best coffee.*

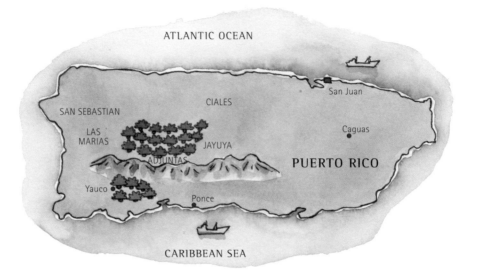

Coffee trees were brought to Puerto Rico from Martinique in 1736, and cultivated by Corsican immigrants. By 1896 Puerto Rico was the sixth leading exporter of coffee in the world, with most of the coffee going to France, Italy, Spain, and, interestingly, Cuba. Although coffee plantations thrived in the nineteenth century, sugar and pharmaceutical products combined with hurricanes and war to push coffee into the background. The industry has now been revived, however, with some highly sought-after coffees being produced.

Puerto Rico is a commonwealth of the United States and, as such, it has a policy of paying a minimum wage. Labor costs are, therefore, high compared with many other coffee-producing countries—only Hawaii and Jamaica face comparable labor costs. Another problem facing the coffee industry is that Puerto Ricans are among the best-educated people in the Caribbean and have appropriately high career expectations.

Today, specialty coffees are exported to the United States, Europe, and Japan. The country's coffee is generally carefully cultivated and has a mild flavor, heavy body, and good aroma. The top of the range coffees are among the best in the world, and the very best are Yauco Selecto and Grand Lares—Yauco is in the southwest of the island and Lares in the south-central area. The best Puerto Rican beans have benefited

---

☕ FLAVOR PROFILE ☕

FLAVOR: full bodied, sophisticated flavor; very aromatic.

SUGGESTED ROAST: medium.

BODY	🫘🫘🫘🫘
ACIDITY	🫘🫘🫘🫘
BALANCE	🫘🫘🫘🫘🫘

Preparing bags of coffee beans for transportation, Puerto Rico.

The Hacienda San Pedro coffee plantation near Jayuya. Puerto Rico boasts some of the finest coffees in the world due to the temperate mountain locations of the plantations.

from the comparative scarcity of Jamaica Blue Mountain, and they can serve as a good alternative when coffee from the neighboring island is unavailable.

Yauco Selecto, which is grown on only three farms in the southwest of the island, is very full flavored, with an intense aroma and a unique aftertaste. It is high in price, but the flavor is the equal of any in the world. The coffee is owned and managed by all the participating farmers in the Yauco region, whose mountain location offers a temperate climate and a longer maturation period—from October to February—together with a good, clay-based soil. Old styles

of arabica beans are grown, and although the bourbon and Puerto Rican varieties give a lower yield than some other kinds, they give uniformly high quality. An ecological, worker-friendly approach to cultivation has been adopted, with low-toxicity chemicals and herbicides used. Employing mixed-use agriculture helps to enrich the soil. Only ripe beans are picked, which requires multiple passes through the coffee trees. The beans are then drum-washed for 48 hours.

Overall, Yauco Selecto is a lovely coffee, with a full flavor and no bitterness. It is rich and fruity and well worth trying to find.

SOUTH AMERICA

BOLIVIA
★

*Coffee from the hedges to
the specialty cup.*

Coffee trees used to be planted in hedges on rural estates to provide floral decoration. Commercial production in Bolivia began in earnest only in the 1950s, and it received a boost from the frost that did so much damage to Brazil's coffee industry in 1975.

The coffee is high grown, at an altitude of between 600 to 2,200 feet (180 and 670 meters) above sea level, and the washed arabica beans are imported mostly by European users as a good blending coffee. The flavor of much of this can have a tendency toward bitterness.

In recent years, Bolivia has developed its own specialty coffee sector, and in 2005 held its second internationally judged Cup of Excellence competition and Internet auction. It netted the winning coffee—from Abricabv, in the Calama region—at many times the current market price.

A narrow road winds through the coffee-growing mountains of Bolivia.

🦋 FLAVOR PROFILE 🦋

FLAVOR: good blending coffee, now developing into specialty.

SUGGESTED ROAST: medium to high.

BODY	🫘🫘🫘
ACIDITY	🫘🫘
BALANCE	🫘🫘

BRAZIL
✶ ✶

*A huge range of coffees from the
world's largest producer.*

As the song says, they do have a lot of coffee in Brazil, and the country has been accurately described as the "giant, the monarch" of the coffee world. There is some Brazilian coffee in virtually all large roasters' blends, and the majority of espresso is based on it.

Today, Brazil's economy is much less dependent on coffee than it was at one time, and it now represents only 8 to 10 percent of the country's gross domestic product. Before World War II, Brazil's share of world production was more than 50 percent; after falling off in the 1990s and then rebounding, it is now nearer to 35 percent. The country's effect on the world of coffee—especially on the price of coffee—is, however, second to none, with frosts and droughts regularly precipitating steep rises in world coffee prices.

Coffee production has become something of a science since coffee trees were introduced to Brazil from French Guyana in 1720. Until 1990 the industry was very tightly regulated and controlled, with stringent interventionist and price-protection measures. Minimum prices to farmers were maintained by the state, which bought up surpluses. At one stage before World War II, surplus stocks amounted to 78 million bags, and these were destroyed by fire or by immersion. Since 1990, a free market has operated. The old Instituto Brasileiro do Café

❦ FLAVOR PROFILE ❦

FLAVOR: many variations available, but generally soft and mild with low acidity.

SUGGESTED ROAST: light to high; many styles and qualities for all uses.

BODY	🫘 🫘 🫘
ACIDITY	🫘 🫘
BALANCE	🫘 🫘 🫘

(IBC) has been replaced by the non-interventionist Secreteria Nacional de Economia and producers are now allowed to negotiate prices directly with exporters. The exporters' activities are, however, regulated by the government, which maintains a register of approved exporters.

To call a coffee "Brazilian" is meaningless, given the huge number of different kinds available. In the coffee market, Brazilian coffee, which is mostly unwashed and sun dried, is called "Brazils" to distinguish it from "Milds," the other arabica category. For mainstream coffee, the beans are further classified by the name of the state in which they were produced and by the port through which they were shipped; the ubiquitous standard grade Santos simply means that it was shipped from the port near São Paulo, probably as a blend of a number of average coffees that arrived at the port at the same time. Although coffee is grown in most of Brazil's 21 states, five of those states—Parana, São Paulo, Minas Gerais, Espirito Santo, and Bahia—produce the vast majority of the total output, with São Paulo and Minas Gerais being responsible for about 55 percent of the overall production.

Given the diversity of the industry, there is a Brazilian coffee to suit all tastes. The northern seaboard area, for example, produces coffee that has the typical iodized flavor reminiscent of the sea, and this kind of coffee—an acquired taste—is sold to North Africa, the Middle East, and to Eastern Europe.

Besides arabica, Brazil produces a large volume of robusta (called conillon and generally grown in the coastal Espirito Santo state), used in mainstream coffee as a filler and as the basis for instant coffee. Traditionally, most Brazilian coffee was blended, but, with the development over the past two decades of a thriving and successful specialty coffee sector, single origin coffees from Brazil are now well established. The Brazil Specialty Coffee Association, which has members in the most important growing regions, represents the top growers and some of the most technically advanced—not to say largest—coffee estates in the world.

The state of Minas Gerais, as an example, has vast, recently created plantations on the

Workers in Brazil spread the coffee beans out on a patio to dry.

Coffee cherries are harvested mechanically on a large plantation, Brazil.

BRAZIL
⁕ ⁕

View over coffee lands in Minas Gerais, Brazil.

plateaus of the central Cerrado area. Here, the huge Daterra estate is both one of the world's largest and a model of high-quality production and processing. Coffees from the more traditional growing areas of the southern part of the same state—estates like Ipanema, Alfenas, and Vista Allegre—routinely turn out some of the region's top coffees. Fazenda da Lagoa and Fazenda Rainha are both estates that feature on specialty coffee retailers' lists, and both have won acclaim for their coffees. Even the northeastern state of Bahia, far from the traditional growing region, has developed fine coffees, along with a computerized system of irrigation that allows huge plots to be tended automatically and picked mechanically.

The coffees in these areas range across the varieties from the traditional Bourbon to new hybrid strains, some of which mature into bright yellow, rather than red, cherries. Many of the advanced estates practice the semi-washed alternative method of preparation, to produce so-called pulped naturals, because the method improves the taste and removes some of the earthy tones of the unwashed naturals.

Organic and ethical coffee is also available from Brazil: the Poco Fundo and Bleu de Brasil are two popular types.

Probably the best indication that coffee has greatly improved in Brazil is the coffee competitions that are organized regularly. These are conducted by Italian espresso roaster Illycaffè, and by the international judges of the Cup of Excellence contest. Both of these have drawn attention to the quality end of the Brazil market, as well as improving prices for the best coffees from this origin.

The best Brazilian coffee may not always be easy to find, because, after the United States, Brazil itself is the largest coffee consumer in the world—and still growing rapidly. Many fine coffees now find their way on to the domestic market, and consumers there are becoming increasingly sophisticated in their tastes.

COLOMBIA
✯ ✯ ✯

Arguably, the largest producer of quality coffee in the world
—silky and aromatic, with a strong, memorable flavor.

Coffee was first introduced to Colombia in 1808, when trees were brought by a clergyman from the French Antilles via Venezuela. Today the country, in normal production years, is the third largest producing country in the world after Brazil and Vietnam, with an annual production of around 12 million 132-pound (60-kilogram) bags. The importance of coffee to the national economy may be gauged from the fact that all cars entering the country are sprayed so that they do not inadvertently introduce diseases that might damage the coffee plants.

Colombian coffee is one of the few origin coffees that is sold all over the world under its own name. With the help of a good product and some clever marketing, no other coffee has achieved that degree of consumer regard for its quality. It is the world's largest exporter of washed arabica beans and very little robusta is grown. More than any other producer, the country has been concerned to develop and

promote its product and industry, and it is this, together with favorable geographical and climatic factors, that has given Colombian coffee its reputation for quality and flavor.

The coffee-producing areas lie among the foothills of the Andes, where the climate is temperate and moist. Colombia has three *cordilleras*—secondary mountain ranges—running through it, north to south, toward the

---

✿ FLAVOR PROFILE ✿

FLAVOR: rich, superbly balanced, and sometimes nutty.

SUGGESTED ROAST: medium to high; all uses.

BODY	🫘 🫘 🫘
ACIDITY	🫘 🫘 🫘
BALANCE	🫘 🫘 🫘 🫘 🫘

Andes proper, and it is along the heights of the *cordilleras* that the coffee is grown. The hilly terrain provides a wide variety of microclimates, which means that the harvesting season can last for almost the whole year, as different plantings ripen at different times. Colombia is also fortunate in that, unlike Brazil, it does not have to worry about the possibility of frost destroying a crop. Most of the country's coffee is grown on plantations organized on modern lines, with the remainder being grown on small, traditionally run farms.

Yields have risen dramatically since the 1960s, but maintaining quality is a priority for the industry, which is managed by the Federación Nacional de Cafeteros (FNC or Fedecafe), founded in 1927. Although it is a private organization, the FNC acts with the government in favor of the growers. In addition to providing services and assistance to farmers, and marketing the coffee, it builds up reserves of money in the good years from farm levies, so that it can maintain price levels to farmers during periods when coffee prices are low. (In some recent years, unfortunately, due to the severity of price falls, even the FNC ran out of funds to support the growers). In general, however, the FNC offers health care and education, builds roads, employs agronomists, carries out research, regulates quality, directly exports a large portion of the total export volume, and employs marketing agents. Respected throughout the coffee industry, it is a model for how such a body can effectively organize a producing country's industry.

The coffee farmers can either sell the entire crop to the FNC at the official minimum price or sell to exporters, who may offer a higher price. In practice, the FNC dominates exports to Europe, while supplies to the United States are more often handled through the private exporters. All exports, however, are subject to a minimum export price, the *reintegro cafetero*.

Colombia is fortunate in having both Atlantic (Caribbean) and Pacific ports—the only South American country to do so—and this helps to keep down transportation and shipping costs. The main production areas are along the central and eastern *cordilleras*, and along the central range the most important plantations are at Medellin, Armenia, and Manizales. Of the three, the coffee from Medellin is thought to be the finest—it has a heavy body, a rich, full flavor, and medium acidity. The three areas are known collectively as MAM, and most of the top-quality Colombian coffee available for export is probably MAM. Coffee from Medellin alone would be so identified and premium prices would be charged. Along the eastern *cordillera*, the best areas are those around Bogotá and, further north, around Bucaramanga. Coffee from Bogotá is less acidic than that from Medellin but equally fine.

Germany was once a large importer of Colombian coffee, bringing in 25 percent of all Colombian exports. One sign of a lower market level in Germany in recent years is the reduction of imports from Colombia in favor of cheaper origins. The United States also takes a good deal of the country's coffee, and the familiar advertisements featuring fictional coffee grower Juan Valdez have made Colombian coffee the best-known origin coffee in America.

The coffee is graded as Supremo; Excelso, a large proportion of which is exported to Germany, and the rest of Europe; and UGQ, which stands for "Unusual Good Quality." It is possible to buy both Excelso and Supremo in many coffee shops. The "official" difference between the two is that Supremo generally has the larger beans. In fact, Supremo tends to come from the more up-to-date producers, where consistent quality is easier to maintain. Excelso is mostly softer and more acidic than Supremo, but both are aromatic coffees, with medium body and good fruit. Colombian coffee is often described as silky; it is one of the best

This family smallholding stands amid rows of coffee trees, Colombia.

balanced of all coffees, and can be enjoyed at any time of the day.

Colombia came on to the specialty coffee scene later than most origins, with the FNC insisting for many years that all of the country's coffee be exported as a few grades. This has now completely changed, as a large number of *ecotopos*, or microclimates, with specific ecological characteristics have been identified. As a result, roasters and consumers are able to sample the wide variety of coffees available from an array of individual estates and farms. Many of these now export directly or through specialty export groups, and the country has had success with organic and sustainable certified coffee as well. Besides Supremo (including Bucaramanga, La Manuela, and Tula) and Excelso (including organic Tatama), look out for Nariño. All of these coffees are now often marketed with details of the region or even the estate where it was grown.

Cup of Excellence, the international coffee competition and Internet auction, holds regular contests for the best coffees in the country, and the winning coffees normally net many times the market price; setting the final seal on the quality aspects of Colombian coffee.

ECUADOR
*

*Perhaps the highest arabica plantations
in the world.*

Arabica trees were first planted in Ecuador as recently as 1952. The coffee is of good quality, especially if it comes from the early June crop and not from a later harvest.

The beans are classified as Galapagos (see the separate section on Galapagos coffees from the islands of the same name) and Gigante, both of which are heavy and large; and as No. 1 and Extra Superior, which are of Scandinavian consumer quality.

The main problem confronting producers is maintaining a consistent quality. Nevertheless, the coffee is generally well balanced, clean, and with an excellent, somewhat individual, aroma.

Ecuador is one of the few countries in South America to produce robusta as well as arabica, although the production of robusta is increasing because of the lack of suitable land for the arabica trees. The best of the arabica coffee comes from the highlands of the Andes, which run in two ranges from north to south

down the center of the country—especially from the Chanchamgo Valley.

Specialty coffee is now being cultivated by a few estates in the country, notably organic Puyango, and Vilcabamba—a coffee grown in so-called "Longevity Valley" because, it is said, an inordinate number of the area's inhabitants live to over 100.

☕ FLAVOR PROFILE ☕

FLAVOR: balanced with vibrant flavors.

SUGGESTED ROAST: medium to high; good blending coffee; versatile.

BODY   🫘🫘

ACIDITY   🫘🫘🫘

BALANCE   🫘🫘🫘🫘

GALAPAGOS ISLANDS
★ ★ ★

*A coffee rarity from the home of
the giant tortoise.*

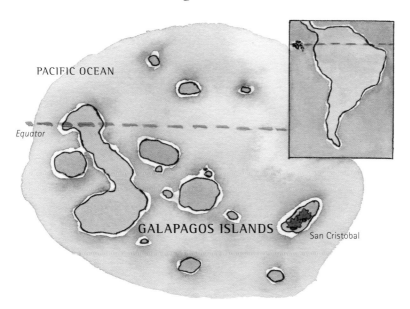

This rare and unusual coffee is of very high quality and is cultivated without the use of chemicals of any kind.

The coffee is grown on San Cristóbal, one of the larger islands in the Pacific archipelago located off Ecuador, and the only island in the group with an abundance of fresh water. Streams, fed by a lagoon known as El Junco, which lies 1,350 feet (410 meters) above sea level, flow down the rocky, volcanic slopes of the island's southerly side. This mineral-rich, fresh water keeps the soil moist and fertile.

In 1875, Manuel J. Cobos, a native of Ecuador, planted about 250 acres (100 hectares) of arabica bourbon coffee on the Hacienda El Cafetal on San Cristóbal. The plantation is located at between 450 to 900 feet (140 to 275 meters) above sea level, which is said to be the atmospheric equivalent of 3,000 to 6,000 feet (915 to 1,830 meters) above sea level on the mainland. These elevations are ideally suited to the growth of strictly hard bean (SHB), with its high acidity, and they are the key to the high quality of the coffee produced there.

As the world's coffee industry evolved to a more volume-oriented business, the small, quality-conscious industry on San Cristóbal fell on hard times, and was eventually abandoned as unprofitable. In the early 1990s, however, the Gonzalez family purchased the Hacienda El

---

🌱 FLAVOR PROFILE 🌱

FLAVOR: rich with a sweet acidity.

SUGGESTED ROAST: full to medium.

BODY	🫘🫘🫘🫘
ACIDITY	🫘🫘🫘
BALANCE	🫘🫘🫘

Cafetal. The unique opportunity offered by the microclimate created by the Humboldt Current, the intense equatorial sun, and the dramatic climate change that occurs as the altitude increases—110°F (43°C) at sea level; 50 to 60°F (10 to 16°C) at 900 feet (275 meters)— encouraged the Gonzalez family to expand the Hacienda El Cafetal.

Since then the plantation has doubled in size, through the recultivation of earlier cultivated ground. Because of their unique role in the history of evolution, the government of Ecuador has made the Galapagos Islands a national park, and no new land may be taken into agricultural use. In addition, the importation and use of fertilizers, pesticides, herbicides, and any other chemicals is strictly prohibited, so Galapagos Island coffee is unofficially, if not officially, categorized as organic.

Annual production of this rarity currently amounts to 3,000 bags, and the Gonzalez family hopes to be able to increase production in the years ahead to as much as 5,000 bags, which is the production limit for the island.

The Galapagos Islands are a national park, so no chemicals may be used in coffee farming.

PERU

★

Good, balanced coffee that can be used in blends.

P eru currently has one of the highest production levels for certified organic coffee of any origin, although quality levels are generally thought to be inconsistent.

The country is one of the great "could be" coffee stories, because given the right economic and political conditions, it could grow excellent coffee. Unfortunately, those conditions are not always available. As much as 98 percent of all Peruvian coffee is grown in the forested areas, and most of the growers are small peasant farmers. The local problems are, however, extensive. Apart from the activities of the Sendero Luminosa ("Shining Path") guerrillas and drug traffickers, the country has recently been hit by very high inflation, which also disrupted the economy.

Peru has benefited, however, as a replacement for roasters in many parts of the world who were finding that neighboring

Colombia's coffee was becoming too expensive. In the mid-1970s, production was around 900,000 bags per year, and this has been steadily increasing to a forecast annual output of about 3.5 million bags for the 2006 to 2007 crop year.

The marketing is a government monopoly, although private exporters operate through

---

🌣 FLAVOR PROFILE 🌣

FLAVOR: balanced with valued acidity.

SUGGESTED ROAST: medium to high; good blending coffee for all uses.

BODY		🫘🫘
ACIDITY		🫘🫘🫘
BALANCE		🫘🫘🫘🫘

A Peruvian woman pulps coffee cherries.

intermediaries to collect coffee grown in the most far-flung areas. The Camera de Exportadores de Café del Peru works to improve quality and aims to instill a "culture" of quality in the 110,000 growers.

The best coffee comes from the regions of Chanchamayo, Cuzco, Norte, and Puno. A large proportion of Peruvian coffee is sold as organic, but it is not always easy to authenticate the growing conditions of all the coffee trees. Organically grown beans can command a 10 to 20 percent premium in terms of price and, given the widespread poverty, it seems entirely likely that farmers cannot afford to buy fertilizers and pesticides. Nevertheless, the problem of verifying the status of the whole crop remains.

Germany and the United States are the most important markets for Peruvian coffee, and it also has customers in Japan, which indicates that at least some of it is of a high standard.

A fair trade worker in Peru displays her freshly picked coffee cherries.

VENEZUELA
✴ ✴

*Wonderfully individual estate-grown coffees are coming
from this oil-rich country.*

Oil used to be thought of as Venezuela's chief export. In fact, although coffee trees were introduced from Martinique as early as 1730, coffee production was virtually abandoned during the oil boom. Recently, however, coffee farms—or *fincas*—have begun to revive, and the old plantings of tipica and bourbon as well as new plantings are laying the basis of a new export industry. At present, most Venezuelan coffee is consumed locally or exported to Europe. However, some of the reestablished estates are beginning to export their coffee themselves.

In early 2006, left-wing president Hugo Chavez tried to force local roasters to pay double the farm price to growers—a move that simply left most of Venezuela's supermarket shelves empty of coffee. When the roasters refused to release the coffee, President Chavez threatened to nationalize the coffee industry, but so far, has not carried out his threat.

The country's coffee industry is untypical in its complexity. There is no doubt that the best coffee-producing area is Táchira state, which is in the southwest, but unfortunately the name "Táchira" tends to be applied indiscriminately to beans from all over the country.

The best names to look out for are Montebello from San Cristóbal de Táchira;

🌑 FLAVOR PROFILE 🌑

FLAVOR: good fruit flavors.

SUGGESTED ROAST: medium to high; many uses.

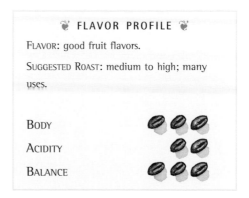

BODY

ACIDITY

BALANCE

Miramar from Rubio de Táchira; Granija from Timote de Merida; and Ala Granija from Santa Ana de Táchira. Other quality names are Maracaibos (which is actually the name of the port through which the coffee is exported); Merida and Trujillo; Santa Filomena; and Cucuta.

Among the estates in Merida, in the foothills of the Andes, is the one belonging to Pablo and Luisa Helena Pulido, which was one of the old farms that had been allowed to decline. Since they took it over in the early 1980s, the Pulido family has been harvesting coffee from the old bourbon plants, as well as extending the farm with new plantings.

The area around Caracas, once famous for its coffee, is also being brought back into production, and another name to look out for is the coffee from tipica plants that is grown on the estate of Jean and Andres Boulton in Turgua.

The flavor of Venezuelan coffee is unlike any other from Latin America. It is light and delicate and has less acidity than is typical, which makes it useful for blending as well as being a flavorsome coffee in its own right.

Coffee plantation near Santa Cruz de Mora, Merida, Venezuela.

AFRICA

ANGOLA
★

*Regeneration of a once-great
coffee industry.*

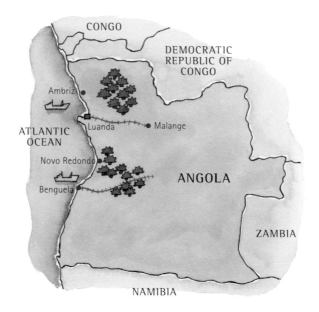

As a Portuguese colony, in the mid-1970s, Angola exported more than 3.5 million bags of coffee each year, of which 98 percent was robusta—and probably the best robusta to come from Africa. It was at one time the fourth largest coffee producer on earth. By 1990, the total production of this strife-torn country had declined to 200,000 bags.

The best-known coffee-producing names from the past are Ambriz, Amboim, and Novo Redondo, which were renowned for their consistent quality. Most of the coffee was exported to the United States and The Netherlands and, of course, to Portugal.

In the past 10 years, the government, with the help of international agencies and the UN, has been working to reestablish the country's coffee industry. Following decades of war between the government and the UNITA rebel forces, moves are under way to resettle coffee farmers displaced by the conflict and encourage production. The International Coffee Organization is involved in one major project, in Kwanza Sul—the province that had been the main coffee-producing region before independence and the war. The project aims to develop and market high-quality robusta for niche markets around the world.

☕ FLAVOR PROFILE ☕

FLAVOR: this coffee has been unavailable in the West for several years but in the past was noted for high acidity.

SUGGESTED ROAST: medium to dark.

BODY	☕☕
ACIDITY	☕☕☕
BALANCE	☕☕

BURUNDI
★ ★

Rich, soft coffee from a relative newcomer.

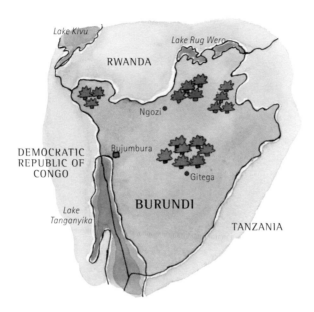

B urundi has one of the most diverse and, in its own way, one of the most successful coffee industries. Coffee trees were introduced by Belgian colonists as recently as 1930, and the coffee is grown on an estimated 800,000 small, traditional farms.

As is the case in most East African origins, Burundi's 35,000 tons of coffee production is sold mostly by auction; although there is some direct sale. Around 96 percent of the coffee produced here is of arabica beans, and the trees in Ngozi are grown at altitudes of more than 4,000 feet (1,200 meters). The coffee has excellent acidity and a very full aroma, and most of the production is exported to the United States, Germany, Finland, and Japan.

The country's main export specialty coffee is called "Ngoma," meaning drum, highlighting the rich musical heritage of the origin, and the fact that drummers from this part of the world, the Master Drummers of Burundi, are famous.

Drummers perform by balancing the drums on their heads and beating on the sides, Burundi.

🫘 FLAVOR PROFILE 🫘

FLAVOR: rich, aromatic with high acidity.

SUGGESTED ROAST: mid and high roast.

BODY	🫘🫘🫘🫘
ACIDITY	🫘🫘🫘
BALANCE	🫘🫘🫘

121

CAMEROON
✶

*A high-roast bean that is
good in espresso.*

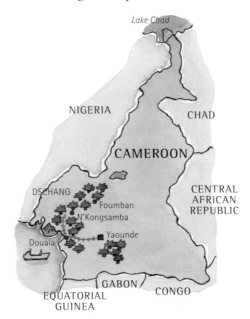

Arabica trees were first cultivated in the Cameroon in 1913. The variety used then was Blue Mountain from Jamaica, but the country now produces equally large quantities of robusta coffee. Much of it is grown on the Western Highlands. The quality and character of the coffee used to be comparable with that from South America, with the best coffee coming from Bamileke and Bamoun in the northwest of the country. There is also some production of elephant bean and longberry, the local version of peaberry.

Like most West African coffee, the country's crop is mainly used for blending or for instant coffee production; there is likely to be little available as a single origin.

Huts in the Mandara Mountains of Cameroon.

☕ FLAVOR PROFILE ☕

FLAVOR: full and soft.

SUGGESTED ROAST: high roast; useful in European espresso.

BODY	🫘 🫘
ACIDITY	🫘 🫘 🫘
BALANCE	🫘 🫘 🫘

DEMOCRATIC REPUBLIC OF CONGO
✳

*Top-quality coffee is beginning to reappear
following the recent war.*

The best Congo coffee is grown in the northeast of the country, especially in the provinces of Oriental and Kivu, and these areas used to produce some of the best peaberry and elephant beans. Top-quality coffee from the country has, sadly, been increasingly difficult to find, especially since the recent war. However, the Democratic Republic of Congo is now a member of the East African Fine Coffees Association (EAFCA) and is once again offering its best produce to the international market—with exports of both arabica and robusta beans to the United States, Italy, and France.

When it can be found, Congo coffee produces an ideal balance of acidity, body, and aroma.

Coffee trees thrive in the mountains of the DRC.

🍃 FLAVOR PROFILE 🍃

FLAVOR: good, acidic coffee; useful for blending.

SUGGESTED ROAST: medium to high.

BODY ☕☕☕

ACIDITY ☕☕☕☕

BALANCE ☕☕☕

ETHIOPIA
★ ★ ★

*The origin with the strongest coffee tradition
still produces some of the best.*

The arabica coffee tree originated in Ethiopia, where it grew wild. In fact, the name "coffee" derives from the Ethiopian region of Kaffa. Many coffee trees still grow in the wild, producing coffee with a somewhat winy flavor and a heavy body. Man's cultivation of the coffee tree is thought to date back to the ninth century, although who was responsible, how, and why remain mysteries. Local legend has it that coffee was first used by monks who needed to stay awake at night to pray.

Today Ethiopia is a significant producer, and quality Ethiopian coffees are among the most unusual in the world—definitely worth seeking out. Around 12 million Ethiopians are dependent on the coffee industry and Ethiopia is Africa's major exporter of arabica beans. The country also has a strong tradition of coffee drinking—unlike most of the other African origins—and the local population consumes a good proportion of Ethiopia's excellent production.

All kinds of cultivation are found, from wild forest-grown trees and semi-developed plots, to traditionally run small plots and modern plantations. Approximately 50 percent of production is grown at more than about 5,000 feet (1,500 meters) above sea level.

A name to look out for is Harrar, for the coffee from this area is among the highest grown of all. Coffee from Harrar is classified as

---

🫘 FLAVOR PROFILE 🫘

FLAVOR: very unusual, rich, fruity, winy, gamey—must be tasted.

SUGGESTED ROAST: medium.

BODY	🫘
ACIDITY	🫘 🫘 🫘 🫘
BALANCE	🫘 🫘 🫘 🫘 🫘

Shortberry and Longberry, and the Longberry is the most keenly sought. It has a soft, winy, almost gamey flavor with a memorable aroma, and it is lightly acidic. Another name to look for is Djimmah, where coffee grows wild at more than 4,000 feet (1,200 meters) and is sold as Limu and Babeka. Coffees from Sidamo, in the center of the country, which are marketed as Yirgacheffe, and from Lekempti, which have a particularly unusual flavor, are other names to remember. Do not be put off by the appearance of beans from Djimmah and Sidamo, which must be among the least attractive of beans— their flavor is excellent. Perhaps the hardest of all Ethiopian coffee beans to find are Yirgacheffes, which are exported to Japan and Europe but until recently were rarely seen in the United States.

It is not easy to describe Ethiopian coffee. The flavor is not punchy or intense, nor does it have the acidity that one looks for in, for example, a Kenyan coffee. It should not be high roasted or it will lose its character.

The first world-famous coffee was Mocha (which is discussed in the entry for Yemen), and the character of this is similar to that of Ethiopian coffee. Good Ethiopian stands comparison with the finest coffees from anywhere, and the best, washed arabica beans will fetch premium prices.

Domestic consumption of coffee is the highest in Africa, and in the countryside it is often drunk with a herb known as *tenadam*, which means "health of Adam." The green beans are roasted over a fire, then pounded with the herb; the whole concoction is then brewed and drunk from very small cups—often as an accompaniment to a small pancake with generous quantities of extra chiles.

The coffee industry is managed by the state-run Coffee Plantation and Development Enterprise, whose control of the market has fallen significantly since liberalization in the

An Ethiopian woman grinds dried coffee beans into powder using a long, wooden pole.

1990s. CPDE and its offshoots have a number of processing plants for coffee in both Addis Ababa and Dire Dawa. A few private export companies have always existed, even when the government was rigorously Marxist, and the independent export sector has become more important recently. The Ethiopian Coffee Exporters Association has 54 active members. The Coffee Unions of Sidamo, Oromia, and Yirgacheffe also export directly when required. The coffee is sold at daily auction, and most is exported to Germany, Scandinavia, the United States, the Middle East, France, and Japan.

IVORY COAST
✯

*Quantity rather than quality from one of
Africa's largest producers.*

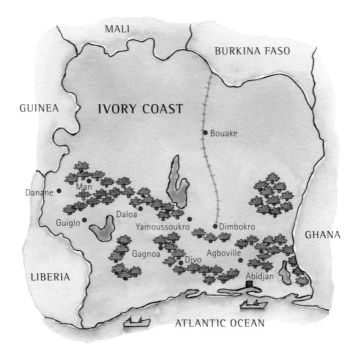

The Ivory Coast has never been a producer of the finest quality coffee, and little of its output comes from arabica trees. The country is included here, however, because in the early 1980s it was the third largest producer in the world, with 5 million bags a year. After several years of civil war at the beginning of the twenty-first century, production has slumped to just over 2 million bags annually.

One of the causes for this decline is the fall in yield, partly because of the general poverty within the country and also because of the aging—and consequently less productive—trees. Lack of investment and a failure to provide long-term management structures have also affected the industry.

At present, 80 percent of the exports find their way to the European Union, especially to France and Italy. If you drink a mass-market coffee in either of these countries, it is more than likely to contain coffee that originated in the Ivory Coast. However, as most of the production is robusta, it does not lend itself to drinking as a single origin.

❦ FLAVOR PROFILE ❦

FLAVOR: full, soft flavor.

SUGGESTED ROAST: dark.

BODY ●●●

ACIDITY ●●

BALANCE ●●●

KENYA
★ ★ ★

One of the finest coffees available—well known for its strong flavor, good aroma, and acidity.

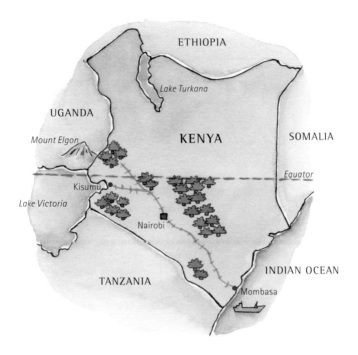

Almost everyone who works in the coffee industry rates Kenyan coffee as one of their favorites. This is because Kenyan coffee has everything we want from a good cup of coffee: a wonderfully satisfying aroma, a fine balance of acidity and body, and excellent fruit. Sadly, in the last decade, production has fallen, and the liberalization of the market has done little to maintain the origin's distinctive quality.

Coffee was introduced to Kenya in the nineteenth century, when Ethiopian coffee was imported into the country via South Yemen. It was not until the early twentieth century, however, that bourbon trees were introduced by the St. Austin Mission.

Most Kenyan coffee grows at 5,000 to 7,000 feet (1,500 to 2,100 meters), and there are two harvests each year. There may be as many as seven passes through the trees to ensure that only the mature berries are taken. The coffee is grown by small farmers, who deliver fresh cherries to cooperative washing stations, which then deliver the parchment coffee to

---

🫘 FLAVOR PROFILE 🫘

FLAVOR: fragrant, sharp, fruity, and full.

SUGGESTED ROAST: medium; the best can be high roasted.

BODY	🫘🫘🫘🫘	
ACIDITY	🫘🫘🫘🫘🫘	
BALANCE	🫘🫘🫘🫘🫘	

cooperative unions (parchment is the last state of the coffee before dehusking). All the coffee is pooled, so no estate-grown coffees are available, and the producer is paid the average price realized for each appropriate quality. This system was meant to reward the best producers for their efforts, but many complained that they did not receive their recompense for the extra effort in preparing one of the world's premium coffees. As a result, the government in the past decade liberalized the market to a degree, removing the export monopoly from the state-run Coffee Board of Kenya and giving it to three private organizations. The government's reduction of the bureaucracy in recent years has unfortunately done little to stem the fall in production of Kenya's coffee, although its best coffees appear to be as sought after as ever.

All the coffee beans are sold at weekly auctions, although at this stage they are still ungraded. The auction house holds the coffee samples and sends them out so that the buyers can judge the price and the quality. The Nairobi auctions are attended by private exporters, and the marketing companies pay the producer the auction price less a marketing charge. The best classifications are: PB, Peaberry; then AA Plus-Plus, AA Plus, AA, AB, and so on down the scale. The best of the coffee is deliciously fragrant and has a bright, rather winy flavor.

The auctions are organized to meet the needs of the blenders. The lot sizes are small—3 to 6 tons—and samples of each lot, along with the grower's mark, are available for tasting. After the auctions, exporters pack together the different styles, qualities, and quantities required by the blenders. This allows the blenders great flexibility, and the quality-conscious Scandinavians and Germans have been among the regular buyers.

The rise and fall of Kenyan coffee is obvious from the figures. In 1969–70, exports totaled 0.8 million bags; by 1985–86, that figure had peaked at 2 million bags. Production in 2005 had dropped to half that amount, at just over 1 million bags. Despite this, Kenyan coffees routinely get very good prices at auction, because the demand for their distinctive quality is still there in many specialty markets.

Look out for AA, the prime Kenyan coffee and one which no self-respecting specialty coffee retailers would be without. Kenya Peaberry also has a strong following.

A Kenyan woman harvests ripe coffee cherries.

MADAGASCAR
★ ★

Arabica begins to appear.

Madagascar is mainly a producer of robusta beans—accounting for around 90 percent of coffee production—but in the past decade has been increasing its production of arabica.

Although the island is a one-party socialist republic, since 1989 the coffee industry has been privatized and freed from many regulations. Total production is high, at around 425,000 bags annually; however, the domestic consumption is also high. As serious coffee-drinkers, the Malagache consume around 40 percent of the island's coffee. France is the main export market, and the robusta is of excellent quality.

Very little arabica from Madagascar has yet been seen in the specialty market, but it is expected that, given the expertise evident in other high-value crops, like vanilla, this could be a good future source of revenue for the country.

☕ FLAVOR PROFILE ☕

FLAVOR: fair acidity and balance.

SUGGESTED ROAST: medium to dark; good for cappuccino.

BODY   🫘🫘

ACIDITY   🫘🫘🫘

BALANCE   🫘🫘🫘🫘🫘

MALAWI
★ ★

Hard to come by, but worth
seeking out.

The product of the former British protectorate of Nyasaland, Malawi's coffee is grown in the highlands along the shores of Lake Malawi, which runs the length of this small, landlocked country.

Coffee is grown in the highlands overlooking the shores of Lake Malawi, Malawi.

The country is one of the members of the select East African Fine Coffees Association (EAFCA), which promotes the region's better coffees. South Africa, Switzerland, Germany, and the United Kingdom are the main customers for Malawi's coffees.

Malawi's main branded export coffee is called Mzuzu, and the country's arabica is described in terms similar to those used for Rwanda: it has a soft, rich flavor, with medium acidity.

🌿 FLAVOR PROFILE 🌿

FLAVOR: light body, suitable for blending.

SUGGESTED ROAST: medium to full medium.

BODY

ACIDITY

BALANCE

RWANDA
★ ★

*A good quality coffee from washed arabica beans with
an unusual rich, full flavor.*

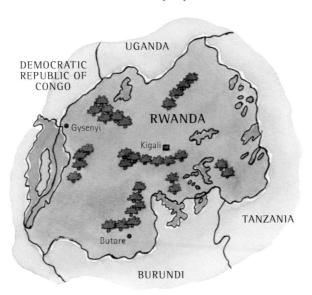

Rwandan coffee production, in the form of washed arabica beans, was of extremely high quality, and the industry was notable (in African terms) until the 1990s, when civil war and genocide resulted in the complete breakdown of society. Fortunately, following these terrible times, the coffee industry has been a way both to rekindle the economy and to give the survivors of the genocide a new purpose.

Rwanda's coffee has come back with strong quality, thanks to the drive of the local growers and also to assistance from developmental sources in the United States and Europe. A number of washing stations have been set up to improve the quality of the coffee, and the results have been good; Rwanda's coffee is routinely finding its way into specialty stores and supermarkets. There are also a number of sustainable and ethical coffees available from this origin, linked in some cases to coffee-growing cooperatives made up primarily of farmers who survived the genocide. Maraba is

one of the best-known regions, and produces an excellent example of the country's arabica.

The flavor of the coffee has been described as "grassy," a characteristic deriving from the tropical climate of the area. The soil is so rich and the climate so conducive to plant growth that the coffee is "forced" or "pressured" and often seems to have grown too fast to give the very top-ranking beans. Nevertheless, the soft, rich flavor is extremely good.

🌰 FLAVOR PROFILE 🌰

FLAVOR: soft, rich, very full.

SUGGESTED ROAST: high roast.

BODY	🫘🫘🫘🫘
ACIDITY	🫘🫘
BALANCE	🫘🫘

ST. HELENA
★★★

Napoleon thought that the only good thing to come from this tiny island was its coffee.

The island of St. Helena, still a British protectorate, lies in the Atlantic Ocean, 1,200 miles (2,000 kilometers) from Africa and 2,200 miles (3,500 kilometers) from Brazil. It has a population of about 5,000, and it is, of course, famous as the island to which Napoleon was exiled in 1815 after the battle of Waterloo. He died there in 1821.

Coffee was first planted on the island in 1732, carried there from Yemen by ship. Although later plantings failed in the 1860s, wild coffee trees grow on the island to this day.

In the mid-1980s, British-born David Henry, whose father was a native of St. Helena, began to develop the island's coffee industry with the aim of producing the best possible coffee. The trees are cultivated in a wholly organic way and there is no mechanization—not even a tractor. Even the trees that are cut down to clear space for new coffee plantings are being recycled.

Henry developed several estates on the island, and his efforts in the last few years have produced some of the world's best—and most expensive—coffees. Most of its very limited supply is quickly snapped up by the super-premium markets in Japan and the United States, but some small amounts are also available on the Internet

---

☕ FLAVOR PROFILE ☕

FLAVOR: rich, sweet coffee.

SUGGESTED ROAST: light to medium.

BODY

ACIDITY

BALANCE

SOUTH AFRICA
✶

Fragrant coffee with less acidity—reminiscent of a Central American bean.

Coffee production in South Africa is concentrated in the northeast of the country, in Natal, between Lesotho and Mozambique, and further north in Transvaal. The southernmost limit is the 30th parallel; further south the danger of frosts makes coffee production impossible.

The trees originated in Kenya and the quality is excellent. In 1975, only about 400 acres (1,000 hectares) were planted with coffee trees, but more recently, a larger area has been cultivated. Most of the coffee produced goes to local consumption.

The coffee is interesting in that it is more like a bean from Central America than from Kenya, the source of the original plants. It is fragrant and pleasingly acidic.

Coffee cherries ripen on a branch.

🫘 FLAVOR PROFILE 🫘

FLAVOR: rich, with good acidity.

SUGGESTED ROAST: low to medium roast.

BODY	🫘🫘🫘
ACIDITY	🫘🫘🫘
BALANCE	🫘🫘

TANZANIA
★ ★

*The best coffees are superb, with wonderfully soft
acidity and an excellent aroma.*

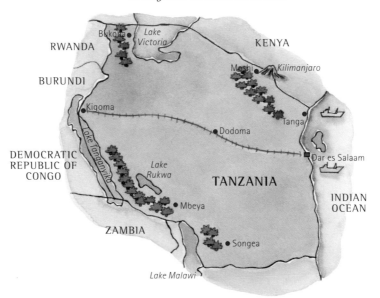

The coffees from Tanzania are an important export item in the nation's economy. There is a good amount of peaberries, which are said to have a more intense flavor than regular beans, and generally the coffee has a bright, sharp character. A good Tanzanian Chagga AA, for example, which comes from the Moshi district near Mount Kilimanjaro, gives a wonderfully full-bodied cup, with a superb fragrance.

Tanzanian coffee has been much better appreciated recently, especially as production in neighboring Kenya fell in the past few years. The country's fine arabicas have succeeded in finding a number of new markets, in addition to the traditional export destination, Japan.

In the past the industry was dominated by estate-grown coffees, but now more than 90 percent is produced by smallholders, many of whom are organized into cooperatives. The most important group of growers is the Kilimanjaro Cooperative Union. Coffee is sold at auction at Moshi to private exporters by the Tanzanian Coffee Marketing Board (TCMB). After some liberalization of the market, private individuals and groups are allowed to buy coffee directly as well. Coffees are often branded Kilimanjaro or Kibo—watch out for these names. Grades are similar to those in Kenya, with AA being at the top, and PB denoting peaberry; both of these are popular and worth looking for.

☕ FLAVOR PROFILE ☕

FLAVOR: full, soft, and with less acidity than Kenyan; lovely completeness and very fulfilling.

SUGGESTED ROAST: medium.

BODY	🫘🫘🫘🫘🫘
ACIDITY	🫘🫘🫘
BALANCE	🫘🫘🫘🫘

UGANDA
★ ★

High hopes and good arabica.

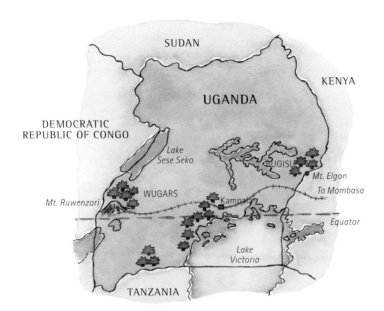

The production of arabica accounts for only 10 percent of Uganda's total coffee, but it is well worth looking out for. The best of the coffee is grown in the northeast, in the area of Mount Elgon and Bugisu, and in the west, near Mount Ruwensori.

The equator passes through Uganda, and the resulting climate has made this country one of the world's main producers of robusta beans. In the 1960s, coffee production stood at 3.5 million bags per year, but, largely because of political problems, this had fallen by the mid-1980s. Now, however, coffee production has risen again and currently stands at about 2.7 million bags. The lack of good roads between the coffee-producing areas and the ports of Mombasa, in Kenya, and Dar es Salaam, in Tanzania, has been a major problem for the industry; as a result, transportation often must be handled by rail.

The monopoly of the former state-run Coffee Marketing Board (CMB) was ended in 1990, and cooperatives have since taken over most of its work. The Uganda Coffee Development Authority (UCDA) is the government agency responsible for coffee, supervising the privatized export sector, the growers, and the traders. It also directs the war on coffee wilt disease, which has taken its toll on the country's production.

The UCDA markets the country's best coffees internationally, and has opened retail outlets for Ugandan coffee in China and Denmark.

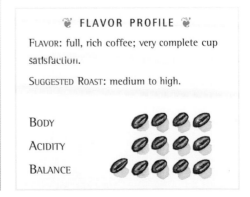

☕ FLAVOR PROFILE ☕

FLAVOR: full, rich coffee; very complete cup satisfaction.

SUGGESTED ROAST: medium to high.

BODY	🫘 🫘 🫘 🫘
ACIDITY	🫘 🫘 🫘 🫘
BALANCE	🫘 🫘 🫘 🫘 🫘

YEMEN
★ ★ ★

*Medium-roast beans with a gamey flavor
come from the home of coffee.*

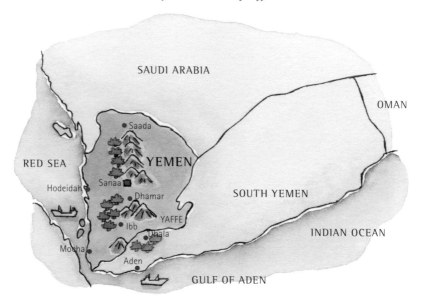

Not really part of Africa, but included here because of its links to Ethiopia, Yemen, even before the sixth century, was exporting plants known as "arabica," (even though the original source of the plants was Ethiopia). The Dutch were responsible for the dispersal of coffee trees throughout the world. Dutch traders traveling east around the Cape of Good Hope sailed up the east coast of Africa as far as Yemen's port of Mocha before they set out on their distant journey to the Indies. In 1696, the Dutch took plants to Ceylon, where plants had already been introduced by the Arabs—perhaps as early as 1500—and then on to Java, in what is now Indonesia.

Yemeni Mocha coffee beans are smaller and more rounded than most, which makes them resemble a peaberry bean—in fact, peaberry beans were sometimes called "Mocha." The finest Mocha is like a Harrar bean from Ethiopia. It has a light body and high acidity, like Kenyan coffee, but combined with an

almost indescribably exotic pungency. The flavor is traditionally a little gamey and chocolaty, so the practice of adding chocolate to coffee was a natural development.

In Yemen, poplar trees are planted to provide the coffee trees with the shade they need. They are grown, as they were in the past, on steep terraces to make the most of the low rainfall and lack of suitable land. In addition to typica

---

🍃 **FLAVOR PROFILE** 🍃

FLAVOR: exotic, winy, pungent, piquant, and unusual—must be tasted.

SUGGESTED ROAST: medium roast.

BODY	🫘 🫘
ACIDITY	🫘 🫘 🫘 🫘
BALANCE	🫘 🫘 🫘

YEMEN
***

A ruined fort stands on a mountaintop near Manakhah, Yemen.

and bourbon plants, about 10 local varieties, descended from the original beans from Ethiopia, are still grown. Even the finest grades, such as Mocha Extra, are dried with the fruit still attached to the bean. The dried husks are often removed in the traditional way—between millstones—which not only makes the beans irregularly shaped, but frequently damages them.

Yemeni coffee can be excellent, soft, and aromatic at its best; unfortunately, consistent quality cannot be guaranteed. The grading of the beans is erratic; although traditionally the best comes from Mattari, with that from Sharki next best, followed by Sanani. Hirazi is another variety that is acclaimed.

The beans, which are naturally low in caffeine, are available for export between December and April. In the past, there have been problems with coffee from the north being adulterated before it was shipped through the southern port of Aden. Only coffee shipped through the port of Hodeida can be definitely regarded as being from the north. Largely because of lack of funds on the part of the growers, the coffee is mostly organic, although not necessarily certified as such.

ZAMBIA
★ ★

A coffee that is a little lighter than Kenyan but with the same attractive East African characteristics.

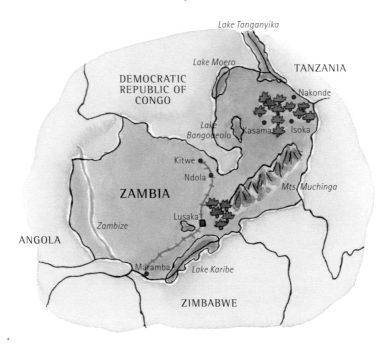

Coffee was brought to Zambia from Kenya and Tanzania in the early years of the twentieth century, and both elephant and peaberry beans are available. A fairly recent exporter of coffee, the country's growers are grouped into a non-profit body, the Zambia Coffee Growers Association, which represents both large and small farmers and promotes Zambia's coffee abroad. The origin currently produces around 7,000 tons of coffee annually.

Moving into specialty coffees in the last few years, Zambia is a successful member of the East African Fine Coffees Association. The top-quality Zambian coffees are good tending to excellent, with a taste somewhat similar to, though lighter than, Kenyan coffee, which it equals in price. It is grown in two areas in the north around Kasama, in the Nakonde and Isoka districts, and near the capital, Lusaka.

Names to look out for, in order to sample the best Zambian coffee, include Munali Estate, Chisoba Estate, Nanga Farms, and Mutuwila Estate. Some ethical coffee is also available from Zambia.

☕ FLAVOR PROFILE ☕

FLAVOR: full; good for blending or, increasingly, drinking on its own.

SUGGESTED ROAST: high roast, good for espresso.

BODY

ACIDITY

BALANCE

ZAMBIA
**

Hand picking ripe coffee cherries at Nanga Farms Plc, in Mazabuka, Southern Province, Zambia.

ZIMBABWE
✷ ✷

*Good quality arabica beans, but supply has
been threatened by unrest.*

Coffee cultivation in Zimbabwe began comparatively recently, in the 1960s, when farmers from South Africa established coffee plantations. Production is concentrated in the country's Eastern Highlands, in the Manicaland and Mashonaland provinces near to the border with Mozambique. The main growing area is around the town of Chipinge, at the southern end of the Eastern Highlands.

One of the most interesting of the coffee producers is the Farfell Coffee Estate, a small, family concern, which produces strictly high-grown, hand-picked, sun-dried beans for the gourmet market. The estate has 170 hectares (almost 420 acres) of arabica trees, which thrive in the good soil, high altitude, and regular rain.

Zimbabwe's Coffee Growers' Association helped set up the Zimbabwe Coffee Mill at Mutare—an operation which processes, grades, and blends a good proportion of the country's coffee for export. Zimbabwe is also a member of the East African Fine Coffees Association.

President Robert Mugabe's controversial land reform policies and the resulting unrest have not directly affected the coffee-growing areas, but they may have affected the market. As a result, it can be difficult to find the coffee, although a number of specialty roasters continue to stock it. In general, Zimbabwean coffee is similar to, and as good as, Kenyan AA, offering a soft, clean, fruit taste. Besides Farfell, look out for Dandoni Estate, and the premium export blend Pinnacle, which has been introduced to the U.S. market.

🫘 FLAVOR PROFILE 🫘

FLAVOR: full, soft, clean with good fruit.

SUGGESTED ROAST: medium.

BODY	🫘🫘🫘
ACIDITY	🫘🫘🫘🫘
BALANCE	🫘🫘🫘

Asia

CHINA
★

Coffee in the home of tea.

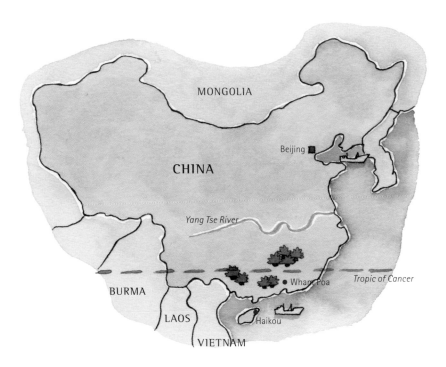

Much of this vast country's coffee requirements are satisfied by imports, but following plantings of the hardy hybrid catimor variety of arabica, mostly in the southern Yunnan province, China can now supply some local roasters and instant coffee suppliers from within its own borders.

The Yunnan Coffee Industrial Corporation (YCIC) is one of the most important purchasers of coffee, and buys the production from over 100 plantations throughout Yunnan province. The majority of coffee production is in the Simao region of the province, which is China's most important growing region.

Robusta is also produced on Hainan Island and in the southern province of Fujian, but these areas are becoming much less important. China was estimated to have produced around 13,000 tons of green coffee in 2001, according to statistics from the U.S. Department of Agriculture.

The country's arabicas, some of which are exported, are said to have light to medium body, with light acidity.

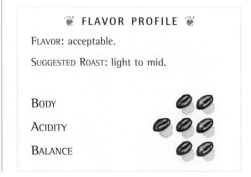

❦ FLAVOR PROFILE ❦
FLAVOR: acceptable.
SUGGESTED ROAST: light to mid.

BODY	
ACIDITY	
BALANCE	

EAST TIMOR
✯ ✯ ✯

*The world's youngest nation
supplies some fine coffee.*

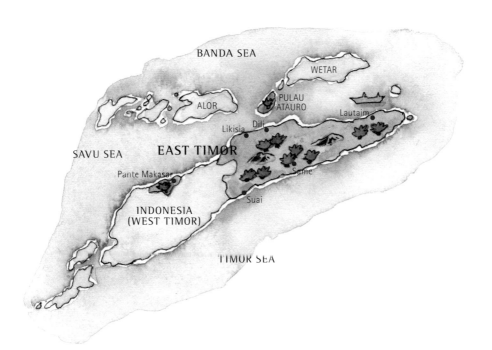

Following its independence in 2002 after 25 years of subjugation by Indonesia, East Timor has emerged as one of the region's best coffee producers, with coffees that show many of the same characteristics as good Sumatras.

The poverty-stricken island nation finds the majority of its income from coffee production, and international agencies are involved in a number of sustainable programs to help East Timor's coffee farmers to produce their crop and to help find suitable markets.

There are three main producing regions: the main area is Ermera, responsible for about half of the production; Ainaro produces the best quality coffee; and Liquiçà, a region situated near the country's capital, Dili. Arabica (80 percent), robusta, and liberica are produced and there is a local hybrid, Timor.

Starbucks is one of the many major customers of East Timor coffee, which is an origin that is increasingly seen in specialty retail outlets—often in organic types that make up a significant proportion of the country's output.

☕ FLAVOR PROFILE ☕

FLAVOR: full bodied, fine fruitiness, and mild acidity.

SUGGESTED ROAST: full medium to Italian.

BODY	●●●●
ACIDITY	●●●
BALANCE	●●●●

INDIA
★ ★

*Coffees in a huge range of flavors and types, including prized
"monsooned" arabicas and sought-after washed robustas.*

Indian coffee has grown by leaps and bounds in the past few years, both in quality and quantity. One main reason is the liberalization of the market in the 1990s, which dramatically reduced the role of the Coffee Board of India as the monopoly exporter.

Under the previous regime, coffee was "pooled" and exports were usually a blend of many different coffees. Since that system was scrapped, the wide range of arabicas and robustas produced in the country have been shown and identified internationally, resulting in better markets and higher production levels for Indian coffee. The specialty movement, too, has developed well, with the formation of the grower group, the Speciality Coffee Association of India. Many of its members can supply coffee directly from their estates.

Karnataka state in the southwest of the country is the main growing region, but good quality coffee is also grown at Tellichery and Malabar in Kerala state, as well as in the Nilgiris,

in Tamil Nadu state, also in the southwest. The crop was recently introduced into the traditional tea-growing region of Assam in the northeast of India, as part of a social program to aid the indigenous farmers there.

The origin is of interest to specialty coffee lovers for several reasons, one of which is the process that is known as "monsooning." In the days when goods and people were transported to and from India under sail, it could take a ship

---

🌢 FLAVOR PROFILE 🌢

FLAVOR: smooth, rich, spicy, full bodied.

SUGGESTED ROAST: medium.

BODY	🫘🫘🫘🫘
ACIDITY	🫘
BALANCE	🫘🫘

INDIA
**

Women sorting coffee beans, India.

several months to travel to Europe. During the journey the green beans were exposed to high levels of humidity, which affected both their flavor and their color, so that by the journey's end the beans had turned from green to a curious shade of yellow.

Customers became used to this, and when steamships shortened the journey time, coffee producers found that their customers still wanted the color and flavor of the voyage-affected beans. In order to reproduce these characteristics, the process of "monsooning" was introduced. The monsoon occurs in the southwest of India in May and June, and during this period the beans are spread, to a depth of 5–8 inches (12–20 centimeters), in special open-sided buildings, where they are left for five days. The beans are raked over from time to time so that every bean is exposed to the air, which has an unusually high degree of humidity at this time of year. They are then loosely packed into bags and stacked so that the monsoon winds can blow around and over the sacks. The sacks are repacked and restacked once a week for seven weeks, until the beans have changed their flavor and color. Finally, the beans are hand-filtered to remove any that have been unaffected by "monsooning," and they are then packed for export. Supplies of monsooned coffee are available from October to February, and this is another mainstay of a good specialty coffee retailer.

Good quality Indian coffee is classified as Arabica Plantation, of which the best grade is A. Monsoon coffees are classified as Monsooned Malabar AA and Monsooned Basanically. There is also some peaberry production.

Some of the world's most sought-after robustas are also from India, where the process of washing has improved their flavor and desirability for roasters, especially those looking for ingredients for a good espresso.

Vegetables are piled up outside the Indian Coffee House in Kottayam, Kerala, India.

INDONESIA
✳ ✳ ✳

*Refreshing and full bodied, arabicas from Indonesia
are some of the world's best.*

Coffee is produced throughout the Indonesia archipelago, and Java is one of the great names of coffee history. The trees were introduced to Indonesia by the Dutch in the mid-seventeenth century (although some authorities think it was earlier than this), and the first coffee from the island of Java was sold in Amsterdam in 1712. However, in 1877 all the plantations were wiped out by coffee rust disease, and robusta trees were imported from Africa to replace the old trees. Today, less than 10 percent of the total coffee production is of arabica beans, and Indonesia is one of the world's most important producers of robusta. Most of the coffee is produced on small plantations, which account for about 90 percent of the total production.

The best growing areas throughout the archipelago are on the islands of Java, Sumatra, Sulawesi, and Flores. Java produces a subtly aromatic coffee that, with its relatively low acidity, is smooth and pleasantly balanced. It is more acidic than the coffee from Sumatra or Sulawesi and has a spicier flavor. The best estates are Blawan, Jambit, Kayumas, and Pankur. Mocha Java, one of the traditional coffee blends, is a mixture of Java with mocha coffee from Yemen.

☕ FLAVOR PROFILE ☕

FLAVOR: Sumatra is heavy bodied, broody, syrupy, and chocolaty—ideal for after dinner; while Java is more earthy, spicier, full bodied, and with mid acidity.

SUGGESTED ROAST: dark medium to dark; good espresso single or blend; excellent in a latte.

BODY   🫘 🫘 🫘 🫘 🫘

ACIDITY   🫘 🫘 🫘

BALANCE   🫘 🫘 🫘

Sumatra, the second largest of the islands, has a rather heavier body, preferred by many connoisseurs. The Mandheling and Ankola beans are especially highly regarded, and the beans from Mandheling have even been described as the most full-bodied arabica in the world.

Sulawesi, the island that lies between Borneo and Papua New Guinea, was formerly called Celebes. The full-bodied Indonesian coffee has a rich flavor and splendid aroma. The best-known beans are from Kalossi, in the south of the island—among labeled brands, look out for Celebes Kalossi—and from Toraja and Rantepao.

Indonesian arabica as a whole is quite strong and warmly flavored, with a rather syrupy quality and often with excellent acidity. Two of the main export markets are Germany and Japan, which is an indication of the high quality of the coffee, but most good specialty retailers will offer Sumatra, Java, and Sulawesi coffees as a standard origin. At their best, the Indonesian arabicas are superb, with a richness that is characteristic of the bean. If you take milk or cream in your coffee, you can add it to a top-quality Indonesian arabica coffee without fear of affecting the flavor. Coffee from these islands suffered the same problems as Indian coffee from Mysore when steamships took over from sail—that is, the customers had grown so used to the effects of the passage on the coffee bean that they were unwilling to accept the "fresher" product. To overcome this, and in an attempt to replicate the conditions produced by the long voyage, the Indonesian government kept the beans in "go-downs" (basic storage huts) for more than a year. Although an acquired taste, Indonesian "passage" or "go-down" coffee, with its individual flavor, is still produced and sold under the trade names Old Government, Old Brown, and Old Java. Matured Old Brown Java is another common coffee found on specialty coffee retailers' stock lists.

Indonesia is also one of the sources of what could be the most unusual coffee on earth, Kopi Luwak. This expensive and rare type is the result of the Luwak or Palm Civet's preference for eating coffee cherries. The beans are partly digested and then excreted by the cat-like animal, and these beans are then collected. Needless to say, with this unusual "processing method," the amount of Kopi Luwak available at any one time is very limited, and the price reflects that rarity.

Women carry baskets in preparation for the coffee harvest, Java, Indonesia.

PHILIPPINES
★

*Rare to find outside the country, as most
of it is consumed domestically.*

Coffee was introduced into the Philippines in the early eighteenth century and by 1880 the country was the fourth largest exporter of coffee in the world. Coffee leaf rust disease had such a devastating effect, sadly, that soon after 1880, the country became a net importer.

Production has been revived, however, and today, after somewhat slow progress, the country has a growing and potentially good quality coffee industry. Although exports are carried out by private companies, about 80 percent of the country's production goes to the top user of coffee on the island, Nestlé. As a result of increasing demand, the government is encouraging production from the coffee growers.

The Philippines is, in fact, one of the very few producers to grow all four varieties of coffee: robusta, liberica, excelsa, and arabica. The island of Mindanao, the second largest and most southerly of the major islands in the group, produces high-grown arabicas of the highest quality; coffee also comes from South Luzon, North Luzon, and Visayas.

The Philippines is, at present, attempting to develop the market for the Palm Civet coffee, Kopi Luwak, trading on its rarity and high price (see the Indonesia section).

❦ FLAVOR PROFILE ❦

FLAVOR: mid; quite full, with some spiciness.

SUGGESTED ROAST: mid to high; good for espresso blends.

BODY	●●●
ACIDITY	●●●
BALANCE	●●●

VIETNAM
★

*From a small producer to a coffee giant—
to an arabica origin?*

Arabica trees were first brought to Vietnam by French missionaries, and between 1865 and 1876 more than 400,000 coffee trees—mostly from Java or La Réunion—were planted around Tonkin.

After the end of the Vietnam war in the 1970s, the government made coffee production one of its top priorities, and developed huge robusta plantations in the central highlands region of the country. With an increase in quality consistency, and the eventual opening of the U.S. market to its products, Vietnam's coffee production boomed in the 1990s—so much so that it rapidly became the world's second largest coffee producer. Production is mostly from small farms, although the state runs a number of large plantations, and handles some processing as well.

Virtually all of this growth was in robusta, and the country supplies all of the world's major markets for blending coffee, and as the raw material for instant coffee.

A very limited amount of arabica is grown so far, although the government is encouraging it as a way of increasing the added value of coffee, which up to now has been mostly mainstream bulk coffee sent to major markets and large processors. Given its success as a robusta producer, there is a good possibility that arabica could follow and specialty retailers will soon stock this origin routinely.

❧ FLAVOR PROFILE ❧

FLAVOR: mid range; good balance.

SUGGESTED ROAST: mid to high; good blending coffee for all uses.

BODY

ACIDITY

BALANCE

150

AUSTRALIA
AND THE
PACIFIC RIM

AUSTRALIA
★★

*Attractive and exotic coffee from a growing and
increasingly appreciated origin.*

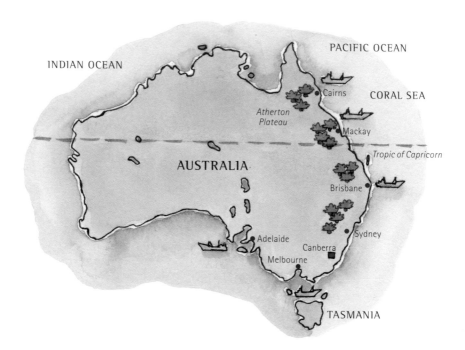

Australia is a surprising country in many ways, and perhaps one of the most surprising aspects is the high-quality coffee that is produced there.

Australian coffee, which is almost entirely from the arabica bourbon variety, is of a very high quality. The flavor is soft, with unusually little bitterness or caffeine. (It is claimed that the coffee grown here contains up to 50 percent less caffeine than that from most other origins.)

From small beginnings, Australia's coffee has successfully established a place for itself in the world's specialty retailers in the past decade. The coffee is grown in two areas of Queensland: in the far north; as well as in an area around Bundaberg in the central and southeast parts of Queensland. The Northern Rivers growing area in northern New South Wales is the farthest south in the world that coffee is grown. Some of the established estates are now well known and appreciated in many markets. These include Skybury, from Queensland, and the technologically advanced Mountain Top from New South Wales.

☕ FLAVOR PROFILE ☕

FLAVOR: soft, with good acidity.

SUGGESTED ROAST: medium.

BODY

ACIDITY

BALANCE

HAWAII
★ ★ ★

*Is this the most beautiful coffee
bean in the world?*

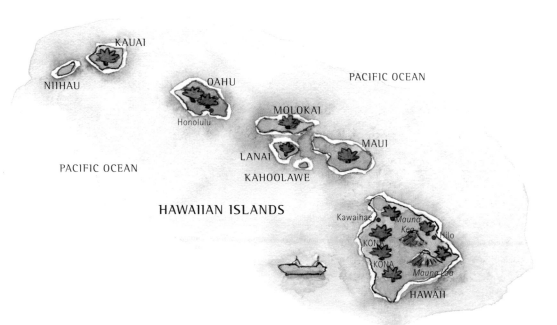

KAUAI

NIIHAU

OAHU

PACIFIC OCEAN

Honolulu

MOLOKAI

MAUI

LANAI

PACIFIC OCEAN

KAHOOLAWE

HAWAIIAN ISLANDS

Kawaihae

Mauna
Kea

Hilo

KONA

KONA

Mauna Loa

HAWAII

The Kona bean has more luster and is more perfectly proportioned than any other coffee bean. The flavor is rich, almost nutty, and is unusually full bodied, with a fine aroma. Some tasters detect cinnamon tones in the smooth, even flavor. Kona coffee from Hawaii may truly be described as luscious.

One of the top specialty coffees in the world, Kona is one of a number of coffees grown in Hawaii, the only U.S. state that grows coffee. The largest market is, naturally, the mainland of the United States, although Kona—and lately other Hawaiian coffees—are finding good markets in specialty outlets all over the world. Of all coffee producers, the Hawaiian industry is among the most tightly regulated and has the highest labor costs, although it does enjoy the best investment levels.

Kona, grown on the "Big Island" of Hawaii, is one coffee that has to compete for space with the demands of the tourist industry. Kona is actually grown on the slopes of Mauna Loa, a volcano in the western Kona district of the

---

☕ FLAVOR PROFILE ☕

FLAVOR: smooth, intense aroma; nutty, luscious.

SUGGESTED ROAST: light to medium.

BODY

ACIDITY

BALANCE

island, in an area about 20 miles (30 kilometers) long. Production is concentrated in the north and south of the region, but not in the center, and the trees were planted in the inhospitable, yet rich, lava on the slopes of the volcano. Although the initial planting was a labor-intensive, difficult operation, the trees in Kona—at least those growing above 300 feet (90 meters)—do not seem to suffer from any disease.

Despite the tornadoes, to which the Hawaiian islands are periodically subject, the climatic conditions would seem to be almost perfect for coffee growing—the right amounts of rain and sun, and no frost. In addition, there is a curious local phenomenon, known as "free shade." It seems that on most days, at about two o'clock in the afternoon, clouds appear and provide the coffee trees with some welcome shade. So good are the conditions, in fact, that Kona produces the highest yield of any arabica plantation in the world, while maintaining its high quality. The average production in Latin America, for example, is 500 to 800 pounds per acre (560 to 900 kilograms per hectare); at Kona, the production averages 2,000 pounds per acre (2,240 kilograms per hectare). Unfortunately for coffee lovers,

however, there are only about 3,000 acres (1,400 hectares) producing Kona coffee.

The best Kona coffee is classified as Extra Fancy, Fancy, and Number One, with estate and organically grown coffees also available. At one time, true Kona was not easy to find, because a great deal of what was available on the market under that name was still made of inferior coffees being passed off as Kona. After a much publicized case of fraud in the 1990s, where Kona was adulterated with cheaper coffees, the authorities and the growers clamped down and tightened the control of Kona marketing and supply. As a result, for the most part, the genuine product is available in reputable specialty coffee retail outlets.

Among the other Hawaiian islands growing coffee are Kauai, which has the largest plantations in the state; Maui, where a number of different coffee varieties have been tested; Molokai, which uses technically advanced irrigation and mechanized harvesting; and Oahu, where the coffee is grown using traditional methods. Besides Kona, other areas on the Big Island—including Kau, Hamakua, and Puna—are coming into production as well.

A coffee plantation on the island of Kauai, which has the largest plantations in Hawaii.

PAPUA NEW GUINEA
✯ ✯

The backdrop for a great modern coffee romance.

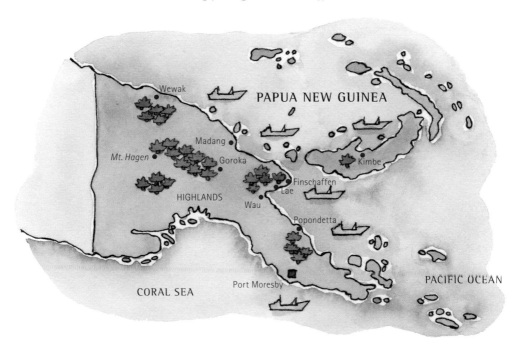

As much as 85 percent of the coffee production in Papua New Guinea (situated on part of the large island of Irian Jaya, north of Australia) comes from small, native farms—many in forest clearings and some so deep in the forests that they are virtually inaccessible. The arabica coffee is almost entirely high grown, being produced at altitudes between 4,265 to 5,905 feet (1,300 and 1,800 meters) above sea level in the Kainantu, Goroka, Mount Hagen, and Wahgi Valley regions, and its high quality is largely due to the altitudes at which so much of it is grown. Papua New Guinea has comparatively little lowland, although robusta beans are grown in some low-lying areas. In addition, most of the native-grown coffees are organic, simply because of the problems and cost of transporting fertilizers and pesticides to the farms (although only a percentage is actually certified organic).

Coffee is a significant element in the country's economy, with about 2 million people involved, directly or indirectly. The government supports the farmers by offering a minimum price at the beginning of each season, and the industry itself is controlled by the Coffee Industry Corporation, which is based in Goroka

---

☕ **FLAVOR PROFILE** ☕

FLAVOR: smooth, intense aroma, nutty, luscious.

SUGGESTED ROAST: light to medium.

BODY   🫘 🫘 🫘

ACIDITY   🫘 🫘

BALANCE   🫘 🫘 🫘 🫘

A smallholder drying coffee in the forested highlands of Papua New Guinea.

in the east of the island. Exports, however, are in the hands of private companies.

The frost that destroyed so much of Brazil's crop in 1975 helped to expand coffee production in Papua New Guinea. A scheme was introduced by the government of Papua New Guinea, whereby village or group landowners would be sponsored to establish plantations of about 50 acres (20 hectares). This measure did much to increase the penetration of coffee cultivation in the local economy.

After a period of quality control problems in the mid-1990s, the Corporation banned the export of the lowest grades and set a compulsory minimum standard for export. This standard was increased again in 2002, and the result is generally higher quality levels for the country's smallholder coffee. These are normally bulked together and called "Y" grade, although the sector has developed two categories—Premium Smallholder Coffees and Village Premium Coffees—which conform to the same standard as the large plantations; look out for names like Elimbari and Red Mountain.

Meanwhile, PNG's estate coffees—Sigri, Bunnum Wao, and Kimmel are three well-known names—are marketed all over the world and appreciated for their excellent acidity, superb flavor, and good body in the cup. The mainstream production of a grade A plantation, however, will have full body, and fairly light acidity, together with great character.

USEFUL LINKS

INSTITUTIONS AND COFFEE BODIES

International Coffee Organization (ICO):
www.ico.org

National Coffee Association of the USA (NCA):
www.ncausa.org

Specialty Coffee Association of America (SCAA):
www.scaa.org

Speciality Coffee Association of Europe (SCAE):
www.scae.com

European Coffee Federation (ECF):
www.ecf-coffee.org

East African Fine Coffees Association (EAFCA):
www.eafca.org

Brazil Specialty Coffee Association (BSCA):
www.bsca.com.br

Colombian Coffee Federation (Fedecafe):
www.cafedecolombia.com

International Trade Centre UNCTAD-GATT (IIC):
www.intracen.org

Coffee Quality Institute (CQI):
www.coffeeinstitute.org

Coffee Science Source:
www.coffeescience.org

SUSTAINABLE AND ETHICAL COFFEE ORGANIZATIONS

International Federation of Organic Agriculture
Movements (IFOAM):
www.ifoam.org

Fairtrade Labelling Organizations International
(FLO):
www.fairtrade.net

TransFair USA:
www.transfairusa.org

Coffee Kids (international charity):
www.coffeekids.org

Rainforest Alliance:
www.rainforest-alliance.org

Utz Kapeh:
www.utzkapeh.org

REFERENCE

Coffee Origins Encyclopedia:
www.supremo.be

CONSUMER ADVICE

www.Coffeegeek.com

www.Home-barista.com

EQUIPMENT RETAIL SITES

www.1st-line.com

www.wholelattelove.com

www.chriscoffee.com

ROASTER AND RETAIL SITES

Whole Foods Market.
www.wholefoodsmarket.com

Dean & DeLuca:
www.deandeluca.com

Starbucks:
www.starbucks.com

F Gaviña & Sons:
www.gavina.com

Allegro:
www.allegrocoffee.com

Batdorf & Bronson:
www.batdorf.com

Intelligentsia:
www.intelligentsiacoffee.com

Stumptown:
www.stumptowncoffee.com

Terroir:
www.terroircoffee.com

Zoka:
www.zokacoffee.com

Victrola:
www.victrolacoffee.com

Espresso Vivace:
www.espressovivace.com

USEFUL LINKS

The Roasterie:
www.theroasterie.com
Gimme Coffee:
www.gimmecoffee.com
Supreme Bean:
www.thesupremebean.com
Kean Coffee:
www.keancoffee.com

Counter Culture Coffee:
www.counterculturecoffee.com
Green Mountain Coffee Roasters:
www.greenmountaincoffee.com
Caribou Coffee:
www.cariboucoffee.com
Peet's Coffee & Tea:
www.peets.com

ACKNOWLEDGMENTS

Betty Attwood, *Speciality Coffee Association of Europe*
Fairfax Coffee Ltd., London
Marshall R Fuss, *Attorney at Law*
Thomas Mitchell, *Strategic Coffee Concepts*

Monmouth Coffee Company, London
Melissa Pugash, *Melissa J Pugash & Associates*
John Sanders, *Hines Public Market Coffee*
Colin Smith, *Smith's Coffee Company*
Mick Wheeler, *Speciality Coffee Association of Europe*

PHOTOGRAPH CREDITS

1 Rolf Adlercreutz / Alamy; 2 Getty Images; 7 Corbis; 8 Stapleton Collection / Corbis; 9 Bo Zaunders / Corbis; 12 Getty Images; 13 Tony Pike Photography; 14 Bettmann / Corbis; 15 North Wind Picture Archives / Alamy; 16 Kennan Ward / Corbis; 18 Juan Carlos Ulate / Reuters / Corbis; 19 Andy Fawkes; 25 Bojan Brecelj / Corbis; 26 The Fairtrade Foundation; 27 Cafedirect plc.; 28 Dave G. Houser / Post-Houserstock / Corbis; 29 Macduff Everton / Corbis; 30 Michael Segal; 33 Michael Segal; 35 David Lees / Corbis; 36 Michael Segal; 39 Hottop USA; 43 Bunn Corporation; 45 Michael Segal; 48 Bunn Corporation; 49 Technivorm; 50 Foodfolio / Alamy; 53 Fairfax Coffee Ltd.; 58 Getty Images; 59 Nestlé Nespresso; 60 Michael Segal; 61 Starbucks Coffee; 62 Dave Bartruff / Corbis; 65 Starbucks Coffee; 67 Jon Hicks / Corbis; 68 Robert Harding World Imagery / Corbis; 69 [b] Swim Ink 2, LLC / Corbis; 69 [t] Richard Klune / Corbis; 70 Michael S. Yamashita / Corbis; 71 Keren Su / Corbis; 72 Reuters / Corbis; 74 Richard Cummins / Corbis; 75 Michael S. Yamashita / Corbis; 76 Starbucks Coffee; 77 Wolfgang Kaehler / Corbis; 79 Pablo Corral V / Corbis; 83 Reuters / Corbis; 85 Juan Carlos Ulate / Reuters / Corbis; 86 Christopher J Morris / Corbis; 87 Lee Karen Stow / Alamy; 89 Andy Fawkes; 91 Michael Segal; 95 Jay Dickman / Corbis; 99 Tim Page / Corbis; 101 Stephanie Maze / Corbis; 102 Tony Arruza / Corbis; 103 & 116 Sue Cunningham Photographic / Alamy; 104 Getty Images; 106 Michael Segal; 107 Michael Segal; 108 Michael Segal; 111 Bo Zaunders / Corbis; 114 Getty Images; 118 Pablo Corral V / Corbis; 119 & 125 Earl & Nazima Kowall / Corbis; 121 Kennan Ward / Corbis; 122 Getty Images; 123 Kennan Ward / Corbis; 128 Tony Pike Photography; 130 Anthony Bannister, Gallo Images / Corbis; 133 Andy Fawkes; 137 Paul C. Pet / Zefa / Corbis; 139 Charles Prager; 141 Chris Lisle / Corbis; 145 Andy Fawkes; 146 Jeremy Horner / Corbis; 148 Ludovic Maisant / Corbis; 151 Mark Richards / Zuma / Corbis; 154 Danny Lehman / Corbis; 156 Papua New Guinea Coffee Industry Corporation.

INDEX

INDEX